NO VACANCY

ultimate
CSI:
CRIME SCENE INVESTIGATION™

LONDON, NEW YORK, MUNICH,
MELBOURNE, AND DELHI

PROJECT EDITOR Laura Gilbert   SENIOR DESIGNERS Dan Bunyan and Lisa Crowe
EDITOR Amy Junor   DESIGNER Jill Bunyan
EDITORIAL ASSISTANT Elizabeth Noble   INDEXER Marian Anderson
CATEGORY PUBLISHER Alex Allan   BRAND MANAGER Lisa Lanzarini
DTP DESIGNER Hanna Ländin   PUBLISHING MANAGER Simon Beecroft
PRODUCTION Rochelle Talary

First published in Great Britain in 2006 by
Dorling Kindersley Limited,
80 Strand, London, WC2R 0RL

06 07 08 09 10 10 9 8 7 6 5 4 3 2 1
CD167 - 09/06

CSI: Crime Scene Investigation
Created by: Anthony E. Zuiker
Executive Produced by: Jerry Bruckheimer, Carol Mendelsohn, Anthony E. Zuiker, Ann Donahue,
Naren Shankar, Cynthia Chvatal, William Petersen, Jonathan Littman

A CIP catalogue record for this book
is available from the British Library

ISBN-10: 1-4053-1672-1
ISBN-13: 978-1-4053-1672-9

Colour reproduction by Media Development and Printing, UK
Printed and bound in Slovakia by Tlaciarne BB s.r.o

Discover more at
www.dk.com

ultimate
CSI:
CRIME SCENE INVESTIGATION™

WRITTEN BY CORINNE MARRINAN
AND STEVE PARKER

CONTENTS

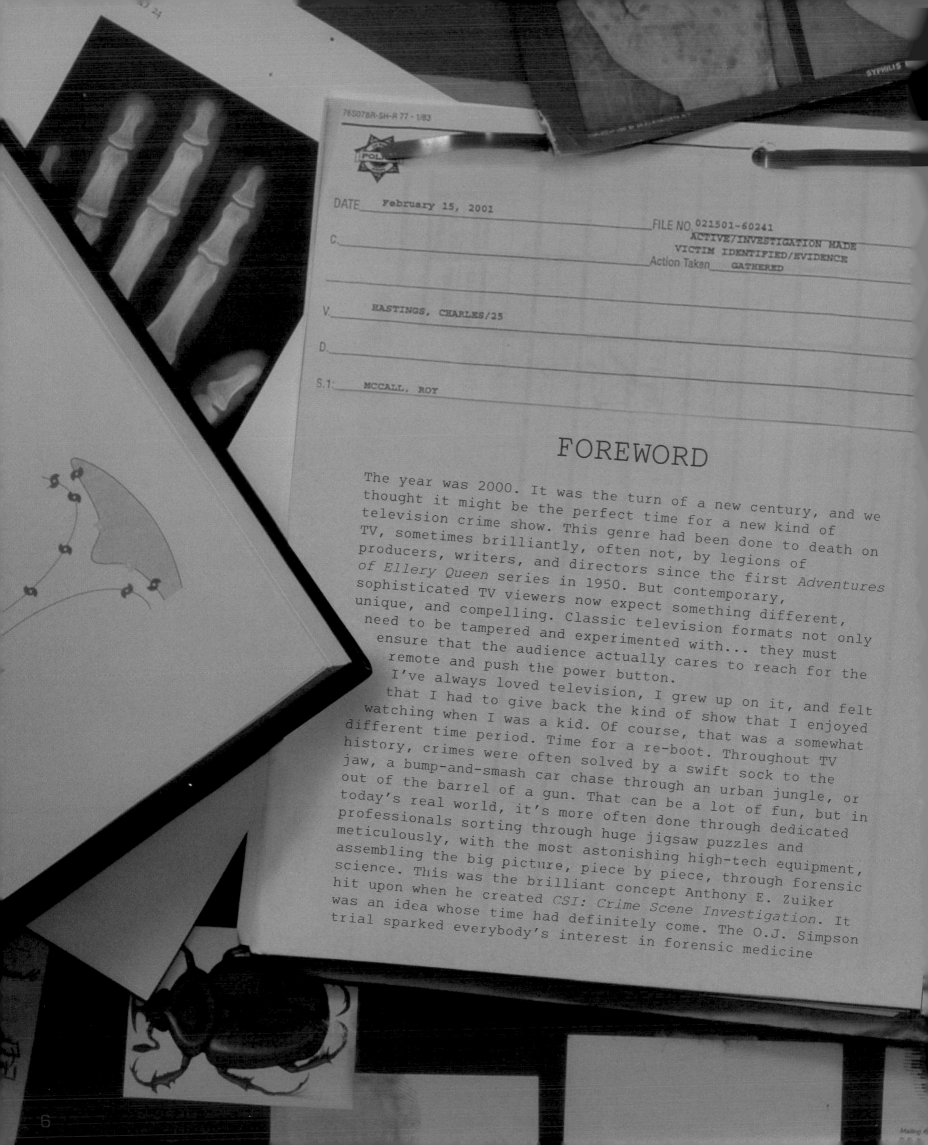

DATE   February 15, 2001

FILE NO. 021501-60241
ACTIVE/INVESTIGATION MADE
VICTIM IDENTIFIED/EVIDENCE
Action Taken___ GATHERED

C._____

V.___ HASTINGS, CHARLES/25 _____

D._____

S.1___ MCCALL, ROY _____

FOREWORD

The year was 2000. It was the turn of a new century, and we thought it might be the perfect time for a new kind of television crime show. This genre had been done to death on TV, sometimes brilliantly, often not, by legions of producers, writers, and directors since the first *Adventures of Ellery Queen* series in 1950. But contemporary, sophisticated TV viewers now expect something different, unique, and compelling. Classic television formats not only need to be tampered and experimented with... they must ensure that the audience actually cares to reach for the remote and push the power button.

I've always loved television, I grew up on it, and felt that I had to give back the kind of show that I enjoyed watching when I was a kid. Of course, that was a somewhat different time period. Time for a re-boot. Throughout TV history, crimes were often solved by a swift sock to the jaw, a bump-and-smash car chase through an urban jungle, or out of the barrel of a gun. That can be a lot of fun, but in today's real world, it's more often done through dedicated professionals sorting through huge jigsaw puzzles and meticulously, with the most astonishing high-tech equipment, assembling the big picture, piece by piece, through forensic science. This was the brilliant concept Anthony E. Zuiker hit upon when he created *CSI: Crime Scene Investigation*. It was an idea whose time had definitely come. The O.J. Simpson trial sparked everybody's interest in forensic medicine because of all the evidence that was being presented, and I think that helped launch our show. From the startling opening images of Las Vegas's bright lights, both glamorous and dangerous, and the power chords of Pete Townshend's appropriately titled classic rocker "Who Are You?," *CSI* boldly announced itself as a show designed to make audiences sit up and take notice. And they did.

"Here comes the nerd squad," one cop says to the other as Gil Grissom and his team approach a crime scene in the pilot episode. What a great notion... build a crime show around a group of people who use brains rather than brawn to solve crimes. Seeing Grissom, as played by William Petersen, on his knees in a suspect's toilet picking up a tiny piece of clipped toenail with a pair of tweezers is hardly a romantic image. But it's a real one. I'm always interested in the process, how you figure out things, getting inside of a world that you're never a part of, and learning all about it. That's what *CSI* is all about. First in *CSI: Crime Scene Investigation*, and then in its equally successful partners, *CSI: Miami* and *CSI: NY*, we take you inside of the characters's lives as professionals, and as human beings, look at the science, and how they do it. On *CSI*, we invite the audience to join the characters in the solving of each mystery. It becomes something of an interactive experience for the viewer, luring them into each episode as amateur criminalists themselves.

We're so proud that *CSI* has become a landmark of American television, hoping that we've innovated the genre and TV in general by injecting qualities usually associated with big-screen movies into small-screen dramas—strong scenarios, mature storylines, and a powerful visual style. At our company, we're in the transportation business. We want to transport you away from your world, and bring you into ours. Tell you a great story, entertain you in a way that can make you laugh, make you cry... and hopefully you'll learn something too. This book will help you become even more a *CSI* insider, since it's co-written by someone who certainly is one herself: the program's associate producer, Corinne Marrinan.

So open the book, and take another step into our world, where crime solving is a science... and the evidence never lies.

Jerry Bruckheimer

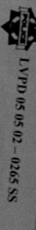

CSI

noun [crime scene investigator] a person who searches for, collects, and preserves evidence. *I hate going out to lunch with you CSIs. You notice everything.—Jim Brass*

ARRIVING AT THE SCENE

THE EMERGENCY SHOUT goes out for CSI to get to the scene! But crime scene investigators may not be the first to arrive. Local police and emergency crews, such as firefighters and paramedics, could be there before CSI. Even so, priorities rarely vary. First, save and preserve life. Victims, suspects, and bystanders all deserve urgent medical treatment—and they may not be who they seem. Obvious suspects should be detained, and witnesses identified and kept separate for later interview. Meantime, the scene is secured with minimal disturbance to potential evidence, which is anything and everything. People are told to touch nothing unless it is vital to save life. Officers present rapidly establish a temporary chain of command until the appointment of an official Senior Investigating Officer.

Tape around the scene leaves plenty of room for maneuvering; for instance, to leave space for earth piles when digging. Later, the tape is preserved as it could have attracted fingerprints or clothing fibres. This could indicate that someone crossed the line, perhaps to tamper with evidence.

FIRST PHOTOGRAPHS

The Medical Examiner makes a quick assessment. Dr. Robbins identifies vantage points where the wide-angle lens captures the general scene layout. Then closer shots record specific points of interest, starting with the body. Macro lenses zoom in for details as small as these words. The key is to chronicle objects in relation to each other before they are removed for study and analysis, and to record immoveable objects for court examination.

Rulers and markers provide a sense of scale and identify a small area. When photos of the marked areas are taken, lights and filters, such as ultraviolet ones, are used to make certain chemical stains glow.

Working Fast
Pouring rain washes away evidence fast. Seconds count. Emergency floodlights are shifted if the normal camera flash cannot penetrate the raindrops. Photos are taken from various angles to capture shadows and because water glare may obscure details from just one viewpoint.

So Many Settings
Each crime scene presents a unique and challenging setting—bedroom to beach, factory to forest. In addition to photographs, the team makes written and audio records of the site, including the precise location on GPS (satellite navigation equipment), time of day, temperature, and general weather conditions. Temporary features such as a howling wind or an obscuring mist could become vital in court. A further visit in a few days may throw up details not noticed in the first survey.

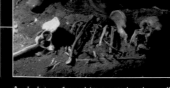
At the shore, lack of mouth foam suggests this victim did not drown.

A skeleton found in wasteland smells of dirt, so decomposition has finished.

Office walls confine a blast to cause greater carnage inside than out.

In woods, a scuba diver is found up a tree following an explosion.

"Want to Call It?"
Nick Stokes and Warrick Brown summarize their initial impressions and begin to work on possible scenarios. Impromptu chats, as well as official conferences, share out evidence and ideas that colleagues could have missed.

Team at the Scene
Gil Grissom and the team survey the crime site and formulate their plans of action. They must interview first arrivals to establish what has been touched, moved, or left, such as footprints. They also start a timed personnel record to log people and what they carry in and out at the scene.

Line abreast, the team join search officers to look for clues and evidence, such as tire marks.

Not Too Close
As the emergency vehicles and CSI trucks arrive, it's tempting to drive right up to the scene. But on soft ground they could be obscuring tire marks or footprints. At night, aimed headlamps provide enough light for the initial work. Gradually, order is established, with one entry and exit point through the crime scene tape. Out come the protective overalls to avoid cross-contamination.

THE FIELD KIT

A STANDARD-LOOKING document case reveals key tools and items that experience shows are best for a CSI's field kit. After each use the kit must be checked carefully. Spent reagents are replenished, batteries recharged, disposables replaced, and the whole kit rendered clean and sterile to avoid contamination at the scene. The CSI truck is usually stocked with camera gear and tripod, a portable fridge to forestall deterioration of samples in hot conditions, and perhaps an extra field kit. In addition to the kit, the investigators take forms, files, rain clothing, boots, and cold-weather protection, such as gloves, hats, and thick coats. They need this protective clothing not just for winter, but for the crime scene in a cold-store or freezer room, for instance.

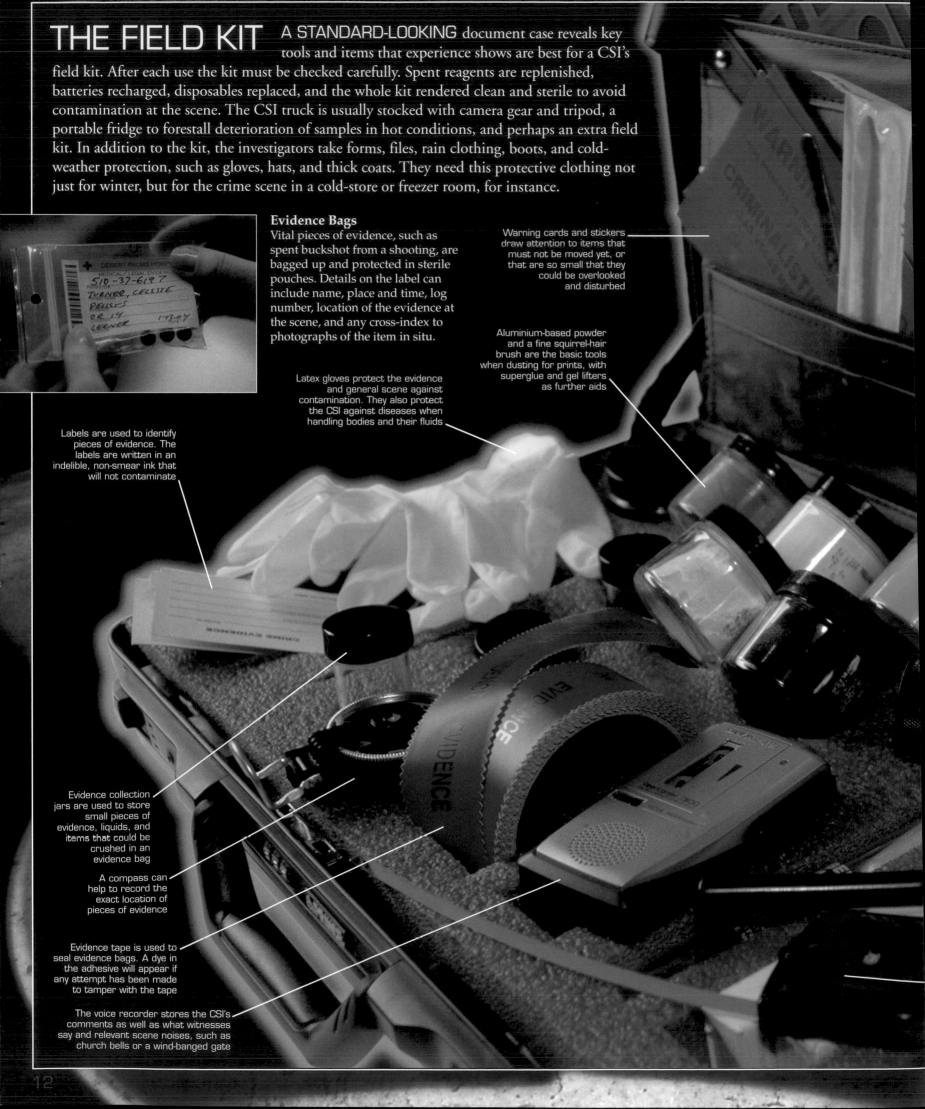

Evidence Bags
Vital pieces of evidence, such as spent buckshot from a shooting, are bagged up and protected in sterile pouches. Details on the label can include name, place and time, log number, location of the evidence at the scene, and any cross-index to photographs of the item in situ.

Warning cards and stickers draw attention to items that must not be moved yet, or that are so small that they could be overlooked and disturbed

Aluminium-based powder and a fine squirrel-hair brush are the basic tools when dusting for prints, with superglue and gel lifters as further aids

Latex gloves protect the evidence and general scene against contamination. They also protect the CSI against diseases when handling bodies and their fluids

Labels are used to identify pieces of evidence. The labels are written in an indelible, non-smear ink that will not contaminate

Evidence collection jars are used to store small pieces of evidence, liquids, and items that could be crushed in an evidence bag

A compass can help to record the exact location of pieces of evidence

Evidence tape is used to seal evidence bags. A dye in the adhesive will appear if any attempt has been made to tamper with the tape

The voice recorder stores the CSI's comments as well as what witnesses say and relevant scene noises, such as church bells or a wind-banged gate

DISPOSABLES

Some parts of the kit are standard surgical issue items, sterile and disposable. Sterile swabs that resemble cotton buds have a multitude of uses: dry, they suck up liquids; moistened with sterile water, they can dab up or rub off samples of stains and fluids, such as saliva from the inner cheek, for DNA analysis.

Architectural templates with scale furniture sizes and shapes are used to sketch the crime scene

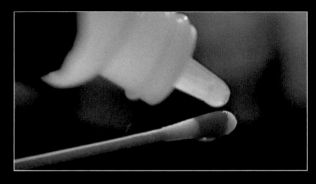

Is it Blood?

The reagent phenolphthalein gives an at-scene indication that a fluid is blood. A swab is moistened, rubbed over the fluid stain, and then phenolphthalein is added. Here, Sara Sidle checks a sample swabbed from a racing robot. The pink color is a positive. It turns out that the robot was the murder weapon.

Gel lifters collect print samples off immoveable objects from fingertips to shoes

Sterile, disposable scalpels are used to slice off small samples or scrape away ingrained material

Different colored dusting powders can be used to contrast with various backgrounds

In the Beam

Flashlights illuminate clues and evidence in dark places, such as under beds and the backs of cupboards and wardrobes. Colored filters are placed over the beam to shine on chemical reagents when CSIs are testing for fluids, stains, and powders.

Modern CSI flashlights have high-power halogen beams and rechargeable batteries. In the dark the flashlights can be used as remote pointers to identify individual elements of the scene.

A magnifier is vital when searching for tiny clues such as fluid spots, powders, or fiber traces, and for assessing fingerprints

A tape measure can be used to measure the distance between evidence, which would not be clear from a photograph

Mini-fingers

Forceps collect small, delicate items gently, without contamination or damage, to place in evidence bags. They can also reach into gaps and corners, as when removing an object from a wound or ear canal. Here, the cola-covered fragment is a piece of a cola bottle that was used as a makeshift silencer at a shooting.

PRINT EVIDENCE

IN HOT CONDITIONS, we sweat. But even when cool, human skin is always producing tiny amounts of sweat, known as insensible perspiration. Certain body surfaces naturally sweat more, like the fingertips. This moistness, coupled with the fingertip patterns of whorled and ridged skin, helps to improve our grip—and leaves a sweaty residue on anything touched. It provides one of forensic science's oldest techniques, established more than a century ago. This is fingerprint comparison, or dactyloscopy (from the Greek "daktylos" meaning "finger" and "skopien" meaning "look at"). No two fingerprints are exactly the same, even on the same person or identical twins. Therefore, a positive fingerprint match means a positive identification. The fainter ridges, creases, and lines on palms can sometimes leave useful prints, as can soles and toes.

Taking prints from corpses can prove difficult, as the skin shrivels and wrinkles. One solution is swab a ridge builder fluid over the finger to "plump up" the ridges of the print temporarily for inked rolling.

Boom Box

A search for clues among scattered debris yields a bomber's detonator. Gil Grissom dusts it for prints using white powder brushed gently over the surface. The powdery particles adhere to the greasy residues left by skin ridges—it's a thumbprint. Different colored powders can be used to contrast with the surface being dusted, such as dark powder on white plastic.

A ridge ending is where the line simply stops

A loop is where ridges curl U-like back on themselves

A birfurcation is where one ridge becomes two

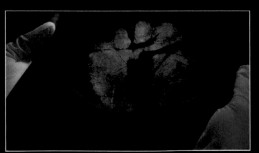

Take-away Prints

After being photographed, prints on immoveable objects can be "lifted" for removal from the scene. Here, Sara Sidle lifts a palm print from a door.

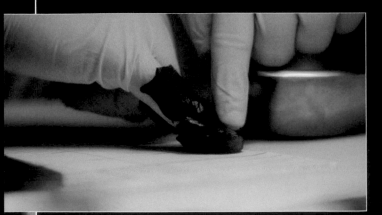

PRINT FEATURES

There are three fundamental fingerprint patterns—arch, loop, and whorl. These are present in different positions and varying proportions in each print. Ridge endings and bifurcations (where the ridge divides into two branches) are also visible. These features are plotted onto a matrix and make every print unique. Instead of using traditional dusting powders, a magnetic "wand" can spread particles based on iron filings. The particles adhere to greasy residues even on some porous surfaces.

Rolling Prints

Fingerprints are taken by inking and rolling fingertips on card. Here, Grissom places a burn victim's skin on his own finger, to obtain correct print pressure.

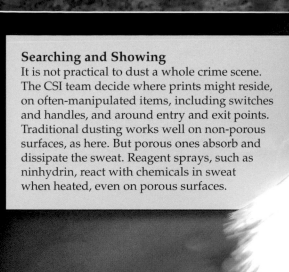

Searching and Showing

It is not practical to dust a whole crime scene. The CSI team decide where prints might reside, on often-manipulated items, including switches and handles, and around entry and exit points. Traditional dusting works well on non-porous surfaces, as here. But porous ones absorb and dissipate the sweat. Reagent sprays, such as ninhydrin, react with chemicals in sweat when heated, even on porous surfaces.

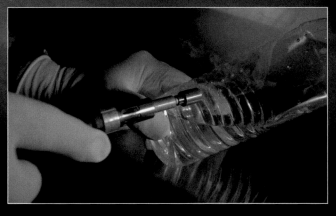

Bottles, cups, and glasses are ideal much-handled, non-porous "print-catchers." Here, the fumes from superglue are puffed into a plastic drinks bottle to reveal any latent prints.

Superglue Tent

Fumes from cyanoacrylates (adhesive compounds known as "superglues") react with sweaty skin residues to reveal prints. If a body is suspected of being handled, a "superglue tent" is built around it, and filled with cyanoacrylate fumes. This shows up latent prints—unseen by the naked eye. It must be done fast, as the prints are degraded by the corpse's body heat and sweat.

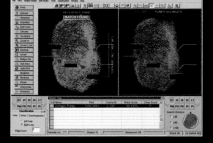

Basic Fingerprint Kit

White fingerprint powder is based on finely ground aluminium and is applied to the area using a soft-hair brush. This brush spreads lightweight particles evenly. Various "lifting" methods remove the powder pattern from immoveable surfaces to mount on acetate or card.

Jar of print powder

AFIS

Prints are scanned into a computer, which characterizes their features and compares them with coded prints in the database. This facility is known as AFIS. From a shortlist of suspects, an expert confirms the final match.

Soft dusting brush made of glassfibers or animal hair

Gel lifters remove dusted prints to take back to the lab for analysis

The transparent cover of a hinge lifter folds back on itself to seal the print

Print-lifting tape for use with backing cards

LEAVING YOUR MARK

SOFT GROUND, such as moist earth, sand, or mud, can be a crime scene boon. It takes all kinds of impressions from shoes, boots, bare feet, and hands to the tire marks of cars, cycles, and giant trucks. It is also perfect for showing up drag furrows and skiddy slips. Early priorities for the CSI team are to identify, label, and photograph the marks, usually with harsh oblique lighting that casts strong, sharp shadows to bring out small undulations. Plaster casts may also be taken. These are then sent to the lab for analysis and comparison. Sometimes a shallow impression or a footwear mark (a pattern of water, soil, or other particles left on a hard surface by the sole) can be "lifted" in the same way as fingerprints, using gel-coated tape.

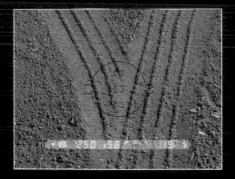

Photographs of these tire tracks show that the vehicle approached in reverse, stopped, and set off forward.

Markers

Tire tracks may run for many meters. They are photographed at wide angle and then in sections, with marker numbers locating each patch within an overall grid or matrix plotted for the whole crime scene. Even if distinctive tread marks are not clear, analysis of the rubber left by skidding can be matched to a manufacturer's particular tire, and possibly to a batch number that went to a certain car maker or tire outlet.

TREAD DETAILS

As a specific model of vehicle rolls off the production line in its thousands, their tires are almost "clones." But wear marks, nicks, and scratches soon make them individual. The amount and pattern of wear gives clues to the mileage the tires have achieved, and on which surfaces, from smooth tarmac to rough track. The degree of "smear" in a print indicates the vehicle's speed and acceleration.

A trapped stone in this tread slot has caused a deeper impression

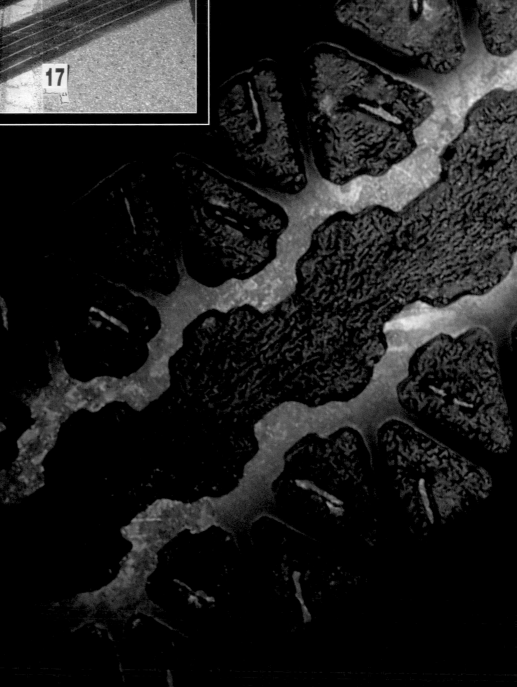

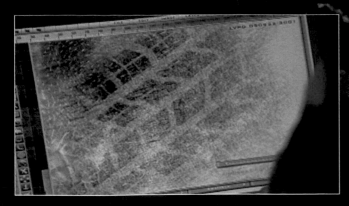

Computer Search

In many countries, vehicle industry manufacturers are required to deposit details such as tire tread designs and paint ingredients into a database, which is available to CSIs. The computer searches the database for the best match in tread size and pattern.

Fatal Sockprint

A man's head is found in a car and the CSI team find bloody sockprints at the victim's storage unit. The suspect tried to avoid leaving shoeprints. But the sockprints have provided ample evidence. As a series, their depth and spacing can indicate the person's gait, whether he or she walked or ran and in which direction, and even the presence of a limp.

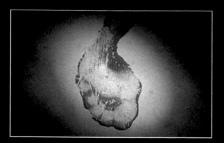

The sockprint provides blood and fibers. Prints can be later recreated using animal blood and butcher's paper.

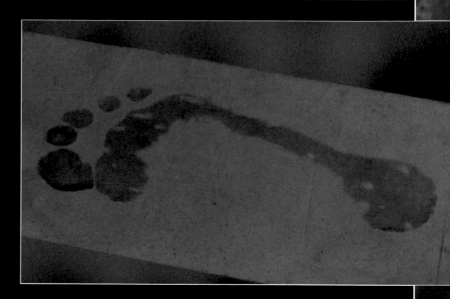

Footprints

A footprint can yield personal features such as the foot's overall size, shape, instep curve, ball depth, and toe length. Foot size can be linked to stature, indicating the height and perhaps, by the fleshy spread, the weight of the maker. After photography, the print can be "lifted."

Impact with the curb has cracked the rubber at the tread edge in a distinctive way

Prints that become shallower at a certain place imply the maker put down a heavy object

Casts

A cast of an impression is taken using plaster-of-paris, "dental stone" (dental plaster), or a pourable, fast-setting material. This can reveal more detail than photos and forms a 3-D copy to compare with shoes.

The length of a print measured on a scale converts to shoe size and so approximate stature of wearer

Shoe Size and Sole Pattern

A deep shoe imprint in wet mud must be blow-dried to remove the excess water for photography and to harden the mud slightly before casting. The sole pattern can be matched to a footwear manufacturers' database. Its wear marks and nicks are compared to the suspect's shoe. This shoe may contain particles trapped in the sole grooves, which microanalysis can link to the ground at the crime scene.

TIMELINE OF A HOMICIDE

THE FIRST MINUTES
The crime scene soon swarms with police officers, and paramedics if a life could be saved. Suspects enter custody and witness interviews begin.

A LIFE ENDS. It looks like unnatural causes. A witness makes an emergency phone call. And a huge investigative process swings rapidly into action. The sequence runs from emergency services, law enforcers, and CSIs, via witness and suspect interrogators, forensics and scientific analysts, to lawyers, legal representatives, and the courtroom. Everyone must proceed with speed and necessity, yet care and caution. There are protocols to follow, agencies to coordinate, permissions to seek, but no time to waste as the CSI team try to record everything and overlook nothing. At the homicide location and back in their labs, the invesitgators play their vital role. The power of forensics can launch a prosecution, confirm guilt, and bring justice for the deceased.

ENTER CSI

CSIs arrive fast to secure the site. From attending officers they hear a summary of events so far, whether evidence has been disturbed, if the body has been identified, and who's in the frame as the killer. There are urgent priorities. Some clues, especially biological, degrade quickly. Outside, rain can wash away footprints, tire tracks, and fluid stains. Even indoors, fingerprints fade and toxins disperse. Quickly the initial searches commence and photography is under way.

CRIME SCENE DO NOT CROSS — CRIME SCENE

Gathering Clues
Some clues leap up at you, but it's not possible to search every location in fingertip detail. The officers discuss possible scenarios. With a mix of experience, logical deduction, and a nose for intuition, they focus their attention at certain sites.

Primary photographs record the scene as found, from various angles and distances, with everything in situ. Sometimes the media are so swift to the scene that press photographers take the first images. These may then be commandeered by CSIs.

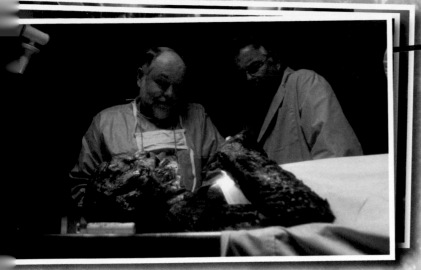

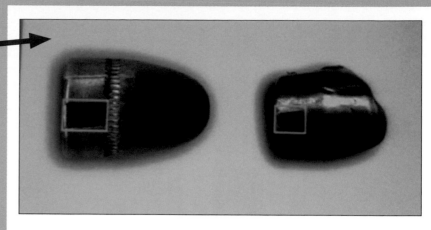

Analyzing Evidence

Each bagged scrap of evidence is a potential crime-solver in the race to identify a suspect. Not only blood, sweat, and tears yield DNA—so do urine, scraps of skin, and other bits of body. Fingerprints are always valuable and micro-examination is made of knives, bullets, and other weapons.

POSTMORTEM
The corpse is a trove of evidence.
After external examination, the
autopsy delves within. Medical records
are obtained for identified victims.

Interviews

Of course "everyone is a suspect"—even the victim, when homicide could be suicide. Interrogators keep their minds open as they question witnesses and suspects. Sometimes the murderer is the person who "discovers" the body, or a close associate of the victim with a cast-iron alibi. Witnesses can skew the investigation by laying false trails. This may be deliberate in order to incriminate the innocent, or accidental, by trying too hard to help, as they recount more than their memories truly recall.

Convincing to Conclusive

It may take minutes, or it could be years, but eventually a vital piece of the jigsaw slots into place. A witness testimony might set the investigators onto a completely new track. Fresh clues are unearthed. A subsequent crime may link back to the homicide. Or a piece of evidence is revisited by the CSI team in a new light.

Case Closed

The CSIs work up their accounts for presentation in court. As part of the prosecution they are bound by legal procedures and court etiquette. As expert witnesses they must be accurate, concise, and watertight, because the defence counsel and its own forensic advisors wait to pick holes and sow doubt. A good day for Gil Grissom and his team is when CSI seals the case.

19

LAS VEGAS
noun [Sp, n., lit., the meadows]
1 City in southeast corner of Nevada, USA.
2 *informal* Sin City. *Is there truly no place left in Las Vegas without slot machines?*—Sara Sidle

GIL GRISSOM

AN ONLY CHILD, Gilbert Grissom was born to a middle-class family on August 17, 1956, in Santa Monica, California. His father taught botany at a local college and passed along his enthusiasm for the natural sciences to his inquisitive son. Consequently, young Gil's idea of playing doctor was to conduct autopsies on small deceased animals found in the local area. Grissom's strong-willed, creative mother was responsible for nurturing her son's love of books. Gil's mother was rendered deaf by the genetic disorder otosclerosis when Gil was still a boy. He became fluent in American Sign Language in order to communicate with her. As an adult, Grissom also began to succumb to this degenerative disease. However, thanks to a surgical procedure and medical treatments, his potentially devastating condition was forestalled.

In order to escape the pressure of a trying case, Grissom has been known to clear his mind with an invigorating reprieve on one of Las Vegas's many rollercoaster rides.

LEADER OF THE PACK

In 2000, Grissom took over as supervisor of the graveyard shift, a close-knit team of five stellar Crime Scene Investigators. Often considered socially inept, Grissom has been criticized by administrators, such as Conrad Ecklie, for being "politically tone deaf." With emotions running high among the staff, this conflict finally came to a head, and Ecklie promoted Catherine Willows to dayshift supervisor, moving Warrick Brown and Nick Stokes under her charge.

Playing office politics has never been Grissom's forte. He has openly resented situations where the FBI has demanded jurisdiction over his cases, or when Sheriff Mobley has applied undue pressure to the lab for results in order to achieve favorable media coverage.

While investigating the murder of a deaf teenager, Grissom used his knowledge of American Sign Language to break down barriers of communication and prejudice.

Wanderlust

Holding a PhD in Biology from UCLA, Grissom is one of only 15 experts in entomology in the US. He is a well-traveled man who, ironically, rarely takes a proper vacation. Grissom's time away from Las Vegas and crime scenes is spent on research trips, attending work-related conventions, and lecturing on entomology.

LV PD

With Friends Like These

During a high-profile case, it emerged that Grissom had been the protégé of Phillip Gerard, a former CSI. Gerard had swapped forensic fieldwork for the more lucrative position of expert consultant in the courtroom. When Gerard used personal information to tarnish the CSI team's credibility, Gil had to stay focused on the evidence to thwart his mentor-turned-nemesis.

Often a mystery to his co-workers, Grissom surprised Greg Sanders by admitting he had once consulted a psychic

Every CSI needs a well-charged illumination device to aid in visual identification

HELD IN ESTEEM

Grissom is a well-respected leader who lives and breathes his job. He is a perfectionist who expects nothing short of excellence from himself and from others around him. Fellow members of the CSI team often find themselves frustrated in trying to win his approval. For a man known for his keen skills of observation and perception, he often struggles to understand the mystery of human emotions. For these reasons, Grissom aspires to an autonomous existence from where he can safely examine the world.

Grissom's philosophy on his work: "If you want to learn about forensic science, master everything else first."

GRISSOM'S OFFICE

FOR A SERIOUS PROFESSIONAL the office is a workaholic's sanctuary, a home away from home. It becomes obvious at first glance that the office of Dr. Gil Grissom is a reflection of his first love: entomology. While the majority of Grissom's menagerie may be mounted or preserved, there are a number of pets that have taken up residence at the CSI lab. An elaborate ant farm, an exotic tarantula, and a team of cockroaches trained for racing are just a few of the species that can be found in Grissom's "zoo." This isn't a mere hobby, but the souvenirs of life spent in the pursuit of knowledge. In addition to natural science, Grissom has also learned to appreciate the natural beauty found in the world, as can be demonstrated by the peculiar assortment of objet d'art adorning his workspace.

ANIMAL MAGNETISM

Fascinated with creatures great and small, young Gil Grissom had spent hours after school studying insects and performing improvised autopsies on deceased cats and birds that he would find in the neighborhood. A lover of all types of animals, Grissom wrote to Roy "King of the Cowboys" Rogers at the age of five and received a certificate granting him and the children of America partial ownership in Rogers's horse, Trigger.

Grissom documents all items in his weird and wonderful collection

At the office and at home, Gil displays his collection of mounted Lepidoptera, the scientific term for "butterfly"

THE MUSEUM OF FISH CO
629
FAMILY FILE NUMBER
KML-32-72
SPECIMENS
SPECIES Syncoryne
LOCALITY Kunamana Pilar
Gamba Gambizee, Congo, Kin.
COLL. Hugh Wilson
DET. BY Hugh Wilson
76F507

THE MUSEUM OF NATURAL REPTILE COLLEC
392
FAMILY FILE NUMBER:
CRL-51-17
SPECIMENS
SPECIES Hydractinia
LOCALITY Fiji South, Fiji Islands, near Dir
CRL-51-17. 8∑316' "N 17∑231' "W
COLL. James Arthur Cook
DET.BY Martin Smith
76F507

THE MUSEUM OF N
REPTILE CO
815
FAMILY FILE NUMBER
DNJ-06-37
SPECIMENS
SPECIES Pennaria
LOCALITY Parcel 132, NW 11
Ranch, 8 mi. W. Billings, Montana
COLL Nigel Lipscum
DET.BY Charles Butcher
76F507

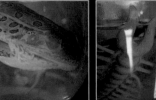 

When Gil offered rookie Holly Gribbs a chocolate-covered grasshopper, she expressed a sentiment felt by many of the CSIs: "No offense, but I don't think I wanna eat anything that's been in this office."

Enigma Wrapped in a Riddle

The contents in Grissom's office are a source of curiosity for many of the lab staff. DNA tech Wendy Simms once asked, "You got anything else in there? Bottle of Tequila? Severed human head?" To which Grissom flatly replied, "I don't like Tequila." What exactly is he hiding in his mini refrigerator anyway? From his private stash, Grissom has been known to produce a homemade blend of "red creeper" powder for challenging moments in the art of fingerprint lifting.

Reptiles Collections
(class: Reptilia)

A vertebrae from the backbone of a horse is one of many curiosities found on Grissom's desk

Precious specimens of insects adorn the entomologist's office like snapshots of old friends

A skilled angler, Grissom repurposed a magnifying glass fly fishing clamp for a desk organizer

GIL GRISSOM
SUPERVISOR

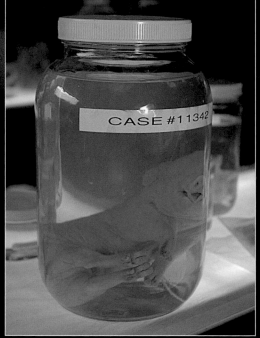

CASE #11342

Gone Fishin'

An avid reader, Grissom's library contains volumes on all subjects, from science to Shakespeare. Above his door Gil used to have the "Fish Board," a fish-shaped pin board displaying "the ones that got away." The photos and newspaper clippings of criminals who eluded the CSI team were a constant reminder to Grissom that cases are never closed until justice is served.

Parting with one of his most prized possessions, Grissom gave "Miss Piggy" to Catherine Willows as an office-warming present after she was promoted to Dayshift Supervisor.

JACKPOT

D R. ROBBINS RECEIVES an unusual package courtesy of the coroner in the small town of Jackpot, Nevada. The box contains the badly decomposed severed head of an unidentified man. Robbins extracts it for examination, noting that the formaldehyde destroys DNA even as it preserves tissue. The mangled head, which was brought out of the forest by a dog, is covered with debris and wounds that suggest an animal attack. But Gil Grissom notices a gash that is definitely man-made—a precise, two-inch cut down the victim's jaw. Grissom deems it necessary to take a field trip to Jackpot to investigate the homicide.

Grissom speaks to the woman whose dog brought the head home. She noticed that the dog was lethargic for several days afterwards, leading Grissom to suspect that the victim was drugged.

CALL OF THE WILD

Grissom finds the sheriff, Alan Brooks, in a local bar in Jackpot. Brooks tries to dismiss the CSI, but Grissom insists on pursuing the investigation. Grissom believes the body is likely to be within a half-mile radius of the woman's house. Using this knowledge plus information from tech David Hodges about the plants found on the head, Grissom begins a search that leads him to the rest of the victim's body, which is found buried up to the shoulders.

Hodges determines that the foliage found on the body is from spruces and fir trees, while the wood fragments are from aspen trees. He also deduces the body's resting place faces north.

Carabid beetles indicate the victim has been dead between four to seven days

Back to School

Grissom recovers a receipt from the victim's pocket for the Western Las Vegas University Campus Store. He faxes it to Catherine Willows, who zeroes in on a book for a sophomore level class that stands out among the mostly freshman titles. Catherine uses this information to identify the victim as Ross Jenson, a WLVU art student.

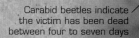

Single White Male

Catherine and Jim Brass question Ross Jenson's roommate, an army cadet named Eric Brooks—Alan Brooks's nephew. Eric says he hasn't see Ross in days, but that it's not uncommon for him to disappear for brief periods of time. Catherine opens the closet door and finds an aspen leaf on the floor.

Blood spatter on the body proves the victim was still alive when he was buried

Old School
While searching for Ross Jenson's SUV, Grissom's high-tech field kit is stolen from his truck. Someone in this town obviously doesn't want Grissom to dig any deeper into this crime. Undeterred by this opposition, he stocks up at a local drug store and improvises his forensic experiments. Using commonly found items, he is able to recover prints from the SUV's steering wheel as well as a shoeprint outside the car.

Mister Wizard
Using a screwdriver, Grissom grinds carbon graphite from a pencil into a fine powder. He then dusts the powder onto the steering wheel using a makeup brush. He shines his flashlight on the wheel to reveal ridges of several fingerprints.

Secret Love
Grissom takes several hairs found in the SUV to the local veterinarian-cum-coroner, who deduces that they are Abyssinian cat hairs. The vet knows the owner—Leland Brooks, the sheriff's brother. The sheriff's opposition to Grissom's investigation suddenly becomes clear: he's been protecting his brother. Internet records show Ross and Leland exchanged romantic e-mails, implying that the two men were involved.

Grissom confronts Sheriff Brooks, who agrees to take Grissom to Leland but asks to speak to Leland first. Grissom waits outside until a shot rings out and narrowly misses him. He rushes into the house to help Brooks subdue an unhinged Leland. The next day, Grissom checks in with the lab and is surprised to learn that Ross had looked up directions to Jackpot before leaving on his trip, suggesting he'd never been before.

IMPRESSIONS—MOTORCYCLE TIRE TRACK
The distinctive imprint of a tire tread belonging to Eric Brooks's motorbike is found near the treads from Ross Jenson's SUV.

If the Shoe Fits
Ross's roommate, Eric, is the son of Leland Brooks—and Ross's killer. The treads of his shoes match the ones Grissom found near Ross's car. After Eric discovered that Ross was having an affair with his father, he followed Ross to Jackpot, drugged him, and buried him alive. Eric wanted Ross to suffer—for choosing his father over him.

ENTOMOLOGY

noun A branch of zoology that deals with insects. *adv* entomologist. *I'm an entomologist.... I know all about bugs.—Gil Grissom*

ENTOMOLOGY

STRICTLY SPEAKING, entomology is the study of insects. But various other bugs and creepy-crawlies do not discriminate as they squirm and munch into a body. So forensic entomology gets involved with mites and ticks (tiny cousins of spiders), worms, and many other minibeasts—especially when the victim is found in water, bloated, and already part-devoured. Each of these parasitic or scavenging species has its preferred habitat, favorite food, and well-documented life cycle. For example, most flies hatch from eggs into maggots or larva; these grow and molt skin regularly in a set number of larval stages called instars, according to the species; then the final instar becomes a hard-cased pupa or chrysalis, from which emerges the adult (imago). All of this happens to a timetable modified by ambient temperature. The result is a wealth of living evidence for the forensic entomologist.

Gil Grissom finds a carpet beetle on a skull, but the body's stage of decomposition contradicts the insect's presence.

A molted (cast-off) cicada larval casing on a hair links a body to a local wood

So Many Flies
Synthesiomyia nudiseta is a cousin of the common housefly (Musca domestica) but lives in cities rather than rural areas. Emerged from its larvae in a corpse, it shows that a victim dumped in woodland initially lay in a city.

Entomology Timeline
Insects tend to arrive on a corpse in a specific order. The presence of their eggs or larvae at various instars gives an entomological timeline. Adjusted for local temperatures and other conditions, this turns back the clock to the day of murder.

ROTTING INTO THE SOIL
In the open air, the first arrivals at the newly deceased are usually flies, such as blowflies, attracted by the first whiffs of decay. They lay eggs which, in summer or centrally heated warmth, hatch and pass through their larval and pupal stages to the next generation of adults within two weeks As the body bloats and starts putrefaction, other types of flies appear, as well as beetles such as rove beetles. At an urban site there may be cockroaches and city ants, and in a rural setting, carrion beetles and wood ants.

Rare Appearance
Cicadas are sap-sucking bugs that live underground for as long as 17 years. Then in one location they all emerge within a few days of each other, chirp loudly, and mate. Finding one can pinpoint time and place with high precision.

Fluids from putrefied eyeballs attract certain kinds of fleshworms

Wriggling maggots and inactive pupae from the scene are kept in jars in temperature-controlled conditions to mimic the crime scene. As the adults emerge, their species can be identified and the timeline confirmed.

Fire ants may scavenge between pupal cases ,which will be monitored for emergence of adults

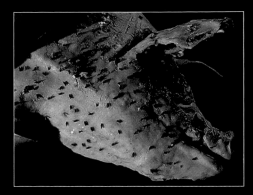

The pig has long been a useful stand-in for a human, being of similar size and organ composition, and readily available. If investigators are puzzled by an entomological oddity, such as a decomposed body in a cool store, they may recreate the situation using a hog carcass and next-generation insects from the original scene.

Pinning Hopes on Flies

Grissom pins fly specimens from a corpse to create a timeline for backdating, and to compare with photographs or actual museum specimens of known identity. The precise species may be identified from body color and wing pattern, but some types of flies are distinguised mainly by the intricacies of their genitalia.

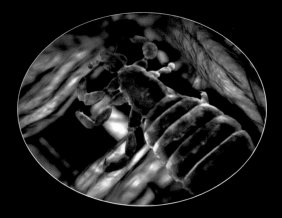

Close examination of a victim's sweater reveals a louse clinging to the fibers. The suspect's car was examined. It had lice—and so did the suspect, the probable source of infestation.

Net recreates the crime scene in a controlled environment

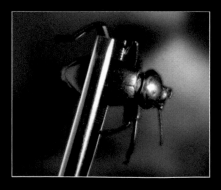

Beetle Pointers

The presence of carabid beetles and second instar fly maggots means a body has lain in the forest for between four and seven days. Rove beetles also turn up at about this time, as do sexton or burying beetles. The species array of insect life can even pinpoint the type of woodland, such as predominantly oak or beech.

THE NET CLOSES IN

A recently deceased man is found at a local "body farm," where the decomposition of corpses is studied using bodies that were donated to science. Only this body isn't one of the residents, it was dumped by a murderer. Autopsy reveals the presence of a maggot commonly found in cows. To refute possible cross contamination, Grissom and Sara use a sample of raw beef under a net cover to observe the metamorphosis of the insect.

The thumbprint from the cassette recorder at the first scene contains red particles, which indicate the presence of latex and lecithin, a chemical found in cooking spray.

A SERIAL KILLER IS LOOSE in Las Vegas, targeting men in their forties and making their deaths look like suicides. Each victim is found in a bathtub with a gunshot wound to the chest and a cassette recorder containing a taped suicide note by his side. The CSI team discovers a link between the murdered men when they learn that all of them share a birthday: August 17. The first victim was born in 1958, the second in 1957, suggesting that the killer is moving backward in time. The victims also happen to share a birthday with Gil Grissom, who was born on August 17, 1956.

NOT WHAT IT SEEMS

The first victim, Royce Harmon, is found dead in his bathtub, swaddled in a sleeping bag with a gunshot wound to the chest. The autopsy confirms that something is amiss in this alleged suicide. The entrance wound in his chest is far too large for a close-range shot, signifying that the bullet was fired too far away for the wound to have been self-inflicted.

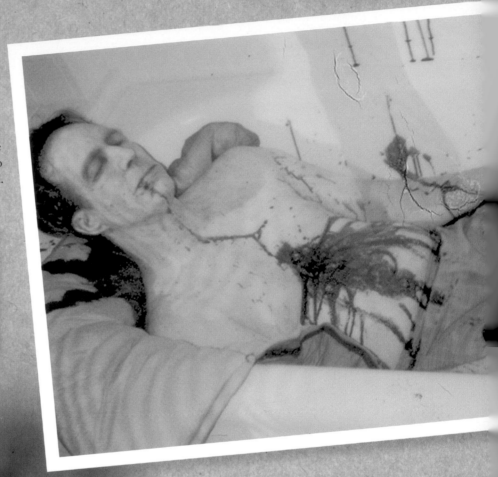

The print from the recorder matches Paul Millander, a manufacturer of Halloween novelty items. Millander maintains his innocence, but admits he works with latex.

LEND ME A HAND

Millander tells Grissom that he created a severed rubber limb made from a mold of his own hand. He sold 10,000 of the popular model the previous Halloween, making his prints accessible to anyone who has a knowledge of forensic science. Looking at the hand, Grissom realizes the killer must have lubricated a similar one with cooking spray to plant the fingerprint on the cassette recorder.

Under My Thumb

Two thumbprints are lifted from the cassette recorder found with the second victim. The first is a match to Millander, presumably from the fake hand, but the second comes back as Grissom's own print. The killer has made it personal.

We Have Nothing

Someone uses the ATM card of the second victim, Stuart Rampler. The footage from the ATM camera shows a homeless man holding a series of cards with drawings on them. Brass tracks down the bum, who describes the man who gave him the cards. The description fits Paul Millander perfectly. Rushing to Millander's warehouse, Gil finds it empty save for an envelope addressed to him with a blank sheet of paper inside.

While Grissom is at the warehouse, Millander pays a visit to the CSI lab. As he exits, he waves into the security camera, a farewell to his nemesis.

HIS HONOR

After Paul Millander claims a third victim, Peter Walker, CSI discovers exactly how he is choosing his victims: all three received speeding tickets in the last year. CSI zeroes in on Douglas Mason, a traffic court judge in Mulberry who is a dead ringer for Millander. Mason claims that Millander is simply his doppelgänger and goes so far as to invite Grissom to his house for dinner. Grissom is convinced that Mason is Millander, and manages to track down Millander's mother, Isabelle.

Isabelle Millander shows Catherine Willows the room of her deceased daughter, Pauline. Catherine recovers baseball cards and a stray hair. Prints off the cards match Paul Millander, while the hair's DNA is female, but also yields trace of testosterone supplements.

EVIDENCE   EVIDENCE   EVIDE

Born a hermaphrodite, Pauline, aged 10, witnessed two men stage her father's murder to look like a suicide. Haunted by the idea that if she had been a boy she could have saved her father, Pauline had sex reassignment surgery at the age of 18.

```
SOLID SUBSTANCE ANALYSIS—ALGINATE
Paul Jr. used his father's hand to make the
impression for an ashtray. He later used the
fingerprints to disguise his secret life.
```

Night Mother

After constructing a life around the need for control, Paul Millander can feel the law closing in on him. Discovering that Millander has escaped authorities using fake identification, Grissom hurries to the home of Isabelle. The woman has been murdered and Paul has shot himself, predictably, in the bathtub. Beside him, a cassette recorder plays a now familiar suicide message.

CATHERINE WILLOWS

Concerned for Grissom's welfare, Catherine followed her boss to a suspect's home and arrived just in time to gun down the killer.

BORN IN LAS VEGAS on March 26, 1963, Catherine Willows was raised by her single mother, Lily, a cocktail waitress and showgirl. Lily's unstable jobs caused them to drift up and down the west coast. Catherine never settled at school and failed to excel despite her razor-sharp mind. She left high school and found work as an exotic dancer to support her boyfriend's rock 'n' roll lifestyle. While dancing, she befriended a regular, Detective Tadero, who got her interested in crime solving and encouraged her to return to school. She graduated from West Las Vegas University in Medical Science, started as an assistant lab tech at LVPD, and worked her way up, under the tutelage of Gil Grissom, to a CSI supervisor.

Head Over Heels

Catherine is ironically surrounded by attractive, brilliant men, like Warrick Brown, at a time when she can least afford to fall for one. Her unorthodox career background and emotional vulnerability put Catherine in an awkward place with her masculine co-workers. But her more recent experience as a powerful, highly qualified professional helps her to stay in control.

Young Catherine was clearing a grand a night working as a stripper at the Paradise Gardens Club. With her earnings, she was able to pay her way through night school and become a CSI.

SELF-MADE WOMAN

Unlike her CSI teammates, Catherine didn't start out with special academic gifts. She was "too smart for her own good" but nobody thought she would amount to much. So, being given a chance to work on Grissom's team was also a chance for Catherine to discover the intelligence and capability she had suppressed. This transformation drove away her feckless husband, Eddie, but it allowed her to build a hopeful future for her daughter, Lindsey.

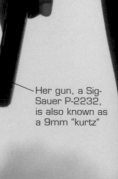

Her gun, a Sig-Sauer P-2232, is also known as a 9mm "kurtz"

A tough life has made a tough woman of Catherine Willows. She is unflappable in the face of gruesome crimes—but being a mother makes her acutely aware of the anguish surrounding child victims.

Into the Depths

Her wild youth taught Catherine to expect the unexpected, but she is still often surprised by the depths of human depravity. Catherine understands the addictive pull of society's underworld, but she has no sympathy for criminals. When she finds purveyors of vice, greed, and cruelty, she wants the guilty dragged out and destroyed.

Catherine's daughter, Lindsey, shares her rebellious blood, but doesn't yet understand her mother's ambition. Lindsey blamed Catherine for the messy divorce that ruined both her life and, far worse, her school performance of *Sleeping Beauty*.

Deadbeat Dad

When her now ex-husband Eddie was brutally murdered, Catherine first responded with steely professionalism, burying the hurt. Many years of conflict and antagonism had tragically ended. However, when Catherine finally broke down and wept over the death of her only child's father, it had an unexpected consequence: it brought her closer to Lindsey.

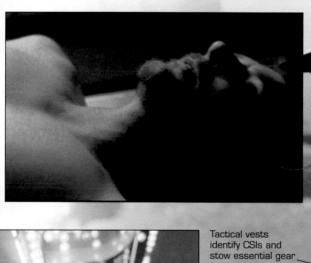

The Bull by the Horns

Catherine is no stranger to extreme physical situations. First, leap into danger, then figure it out: she's the first to volunteer when it's time to pilot a dragster, shimmy beneath a collapsed building, or jump in the water when someone needs saving. This dynamic, hands-on approach distinguishes Catherine from her more cerebral, laboratory-oriented counterparts.

Tactical vests identify CSIs and stow essential gear

Catherine discovered her long-absent father was, in fact, old family "friend" and casino mogul, Sam Braun. After years of grappling with having a criminally attached rogue as a dad, she lost him altogether when he was gunned down by his adversaries.

IT'S BUSINESS AS USUAL inside the First Monument Bank, until a team of four armed men burst in wearing masks and black face paint. One man obscures the surveillance cameras while another rounds up the hostages, including off-duty Las Vegas police office Cyrus Lockwood. The two other men take the bank's manager downstairs and force him to open the safe deposit vault. A strategic explosion in the vault rattles the building. A young mother panics and is threatened by one of the criminals. Lockwood intervenes with his firearm, but before he can get a shot off, a bullet takes him down. As police squad cars arrive, shots are fired disabling the police vehicles and the masked men make their escape in a getaway van.

The video camera lenses are smeared with a greasy black substance, which Trace determines to be camouflage face paint used by the military. An eyelash found embedded in the cream is sent to DNA for analysis.

BIRD ON A WIRE

Gil Grissom notices that heckle marks on the broken window indicate Lockwood's fatal bullet came from outside the bank. Using a dummy and lasers to determine the angle of trajectory, Nick Stokes traces the origin of the bullet to a building across the street. There he finds the sniper's deserted perch by a window and trace of GSR (gunshot residue). Bobby Dawson in Ballistics confirms that the gun used in the murder was an M-1A, and the range at which Lockwood was killed proves the shooter was a skilled marksman.

Mystery Loot

While sifting through the debris in the obliterated vault, Grissom notices that the placement of the four charges is focused around a specific safe deposit box. The construction of the explosives and detonator indicate a technician with military training.

Collateral Damage

Detective Lockwood came from brave stock. His father was a firefighter who also died a hero's death. Losing one of their own always hits the department hard. While processing the bank, another murder is reported: the getaway van is found with the driver strangled behind the wheel.

Up in Smoke

Sara Sidle reassembles the vault rubble and finds that only safe deposit box number 729 is missing. The box is registered to recently deceased Benny Murdock, a longtime employee of casino mogul Sam Braun. Meanwhile, a fingerprint off the detonator is a match to Robert Rubio, former soldier and a security expert at the Rampart Casino, also owned by Sam Braun. SWAT leads the way into Rubio's residence, where CSI finds the charred remains of box 729.

Cold Case

In the box is a shred of a multicolored chiffon fabric and two blood samples. DNA from the first sample comes back unknown. The other is a match to Vivian Verona, a cocktail waitress who was stabbed to death at one of Sam Braun's casinos.

In the Wind

Three men are executed in the desert. While processing the scene, Grissom catches sight of a silk scarf blowing in the breeze, which matches the fabric found in the box. Grissom surmises Verona's unusual stab wounds could have been inflicted by scissors, a weapon of opportunity.

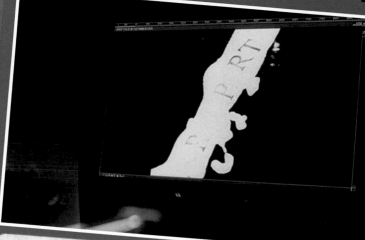

EVIDENCE EVIDENCE EVIDENCE EV

A/V ANALYSIS—SCISSORS
Something had been wrapped in the scarf. The computer reconstructs the stain pattern. By enhancing the detail, an image of a pair of scissors appears, engraved with the word "Rampart."

Cutting Crew

The body of Vivian Verona was discovered inside one of Braun's casinos on the day the building was to be demolished. Grissom notes that the scarf that matches her uniform was not present when the crime scene photo was taken.

The LVPD looks on as cop killer Robert Rubio is taken into custody. Rubio chooses death row over ratting out his employer. "I'll live longer," he says.

Dirty Little Secrets

Braun claims Murdock killed Verona with scissors and then hid them in the box. Braun then hired a crew to retrieve the scissors and make them disappear. Seeing through the lie and wanting to confirm whether she is related to Braun, Catherine Willows has the unidentified blood sample from the box tested against her own. It reveals that Braun is both her biological father, and a murderer.

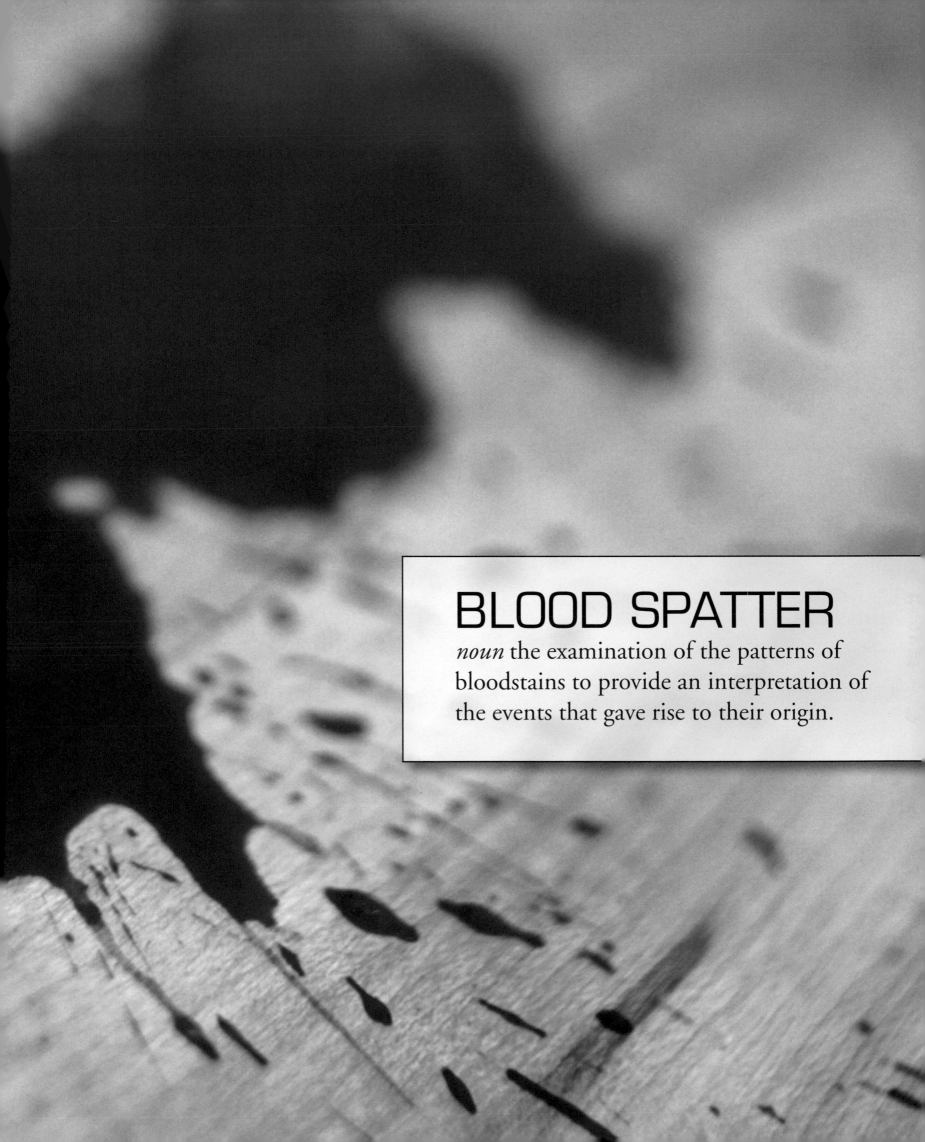

BLOOD SPATTER

noun the examination of the patterns of bloodstains to provide an interpretation of the events that gave rise to their origin.

BLOOD SPATTER EVIDENCE

SIS KNOW THAT bloodstains are primary evidence at any crime scene. Not only can the blood itself be matched to an individual by typing and DNA profiling, but the pattern of its spread yields immense amounts of information. In almost any violent assault some blood is spilt, and even bleach cannot totally erase its traces. The pattern of spots, splashes, and spatters provide clues such as the type of weapon used, the force of a physical blow or bullet impact, how many times this happens, and even the position, height, and handedness (left or right) of the attacker, according to how the spatter lines curve. If blood is suspected but not obvious, a high-power short-wavelength violet light source or reagent sprays, such as luminol or fluorescin, can reveal all.

Radiating lines or spats of blood drops indicate spray from a central point. Configuring strings or pieces of tape along these lines should track back to the origin. Sets of different colored strings distinguish several spray events.

Spatter Patterns

Patterns involve the arrangement of spots, their size and distance apart, how they smear, and in which direction. Fresh spatters on a vertical surface of a moveable object run down under gravity. But if the object moves, the smear direction can confuse things.

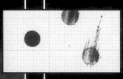

Circles show that the blood arrived from nearby at right angles without running, so the surface was probably horizontal.

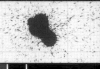

Crenellations have widespread splashes around the central zone, indicating the blood was thrown or fell some distance.

Spurts show a forceful oblique impact, usually to an artery, where the main jet creates tiny droplets around the central site.

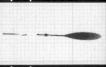

Tailed ellipses suggest drops striking at a low angle, usually less than 30 degrees.

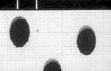

Ellipses of blood are often from an oblique impact.

Swabbing

Blood needed for urgent lab analysis is swabbed from areas that are not vital for interpreting the pattern of stain and spatter. The thickness or coagulation stage of the blood is roughly determined from the way it mops up and soaks into the swab. This denotes how fresh it is, taking into account factors such as temperature and air currents from wind or fans.

Clean-edged circle on the floor shows blood impacting from directly above

MULTIPLE PATTERNS

In reality, blood patterns are often a combination of various spatters, drops, and pools. A large pool implies that the victim was unconscious, but still alive, as the blood pumped or oozed from the wound and spread slowly. After death, the flow ceases except for the pull of gravity, and then the blood itself becomes too clotted or coagulated, and too viscous to run or drip.

Blood trails vary from tiny drips far apart from a minor wound to an obvious long smear where a body has been dragged. The stage of drying and coagulation shows how quickly the hauling took place to within an accuracy of less than a minute, and in how many stages, giving clues to the puller's strength.

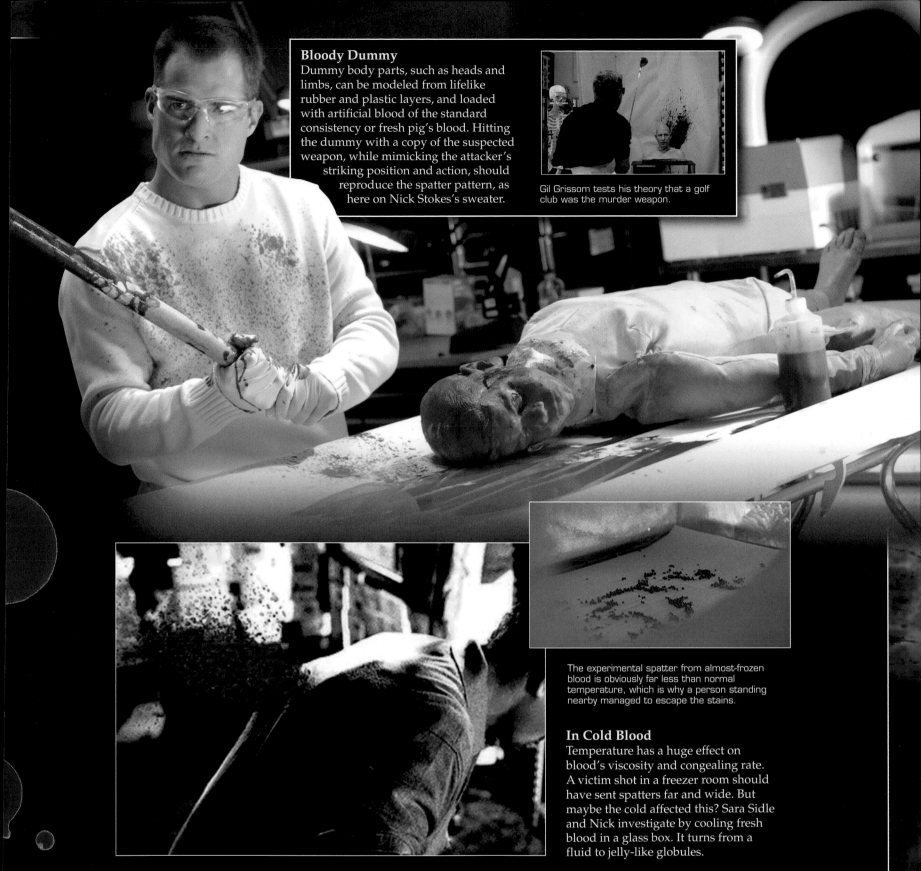

Bloody Dummy

Dummy body parts, such as heads and limbs, can be modeled from lifelike rubber and plastic layers, and loaded with artificial blood of the standard consistency or fresh pig's blood. Hitting the dummy with a copy of the suspected weapon, while mimicking the attacker's striking position and action, should reproduce the spatter pattern, as here on Nick Stokes's sweater.

Gil Grissom tests his theory that a golf club was the murder weapon.

The experimental spatter from almost-frozen blood is obviously far less than normal temperature, which is why a person standing nearby managed to escape the stains.

In Cold Blood

Temperature has a huge effect on blood's viscosity and congealing rate. A victim shot in a freezer room should have sent spatters far and wide. But maybe the cold affected this? Sara Sidle and Nick investigate by cooling fresh blood in a glass box. It turns from a fluid to jelly-like globules.

A blood-coated weapon swung back fast after impact releases a linear "sheet" of blood that splashes like a cascade onto the window. Rivulets drip down, indicating the quantity of blood and its freshness.

Deadly Silhouette

Objects that are stood in the line of spray and spatter leave a blood-free "shadow" on any surface behind them. In some cases the contours reflect the outline of a person, perhaps holding a weapon or an object as a shield, and how far they were from the surface at the time. From the void's shape, the CSI team glean clues as to who or what they should look for to test for the presence of blood.

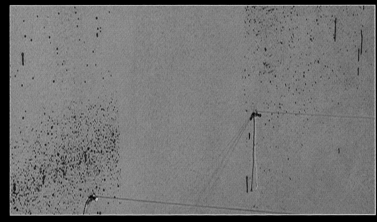

Paramedics rush to revive Mathers, having only seconds to reverse the process. With vital signs restored, he awaits the next ruling on his fate.

BLUE PAINT KILLER

CASE#03-305A-506

J OHN MATHERS'S time is up. The state of Nevada is preparing him for death by lethal injection for the murder of Charlene Roth. Just as the drugs begin to take effect, he is granted a last minute stay of execution. The case lands back in the lap of Catherine Willows, who was a rookie when she put away Mathers 15 years prior. DNA technology that wasn't available at the time can now be utilized to analyze hairs that were recovered from Roth's corpse in 1987. The evidence is expedited to the US Department of Justice lab for mitochondrial DNA testing. Mathers, a campus security guard, is also suspected of killing two other young women who, like Roth, were students at Western Las Vegas University.

CASE OPEN

Catherine reopens the old case files to review the crime scene photos of Charlene Roth. The body of the student was found wrapped in a black trash bag. Her hands were bound with plastic cord and had traces of blue paint on them. Meanwhile, the body of another student, Debbie Reston, is found on the WLVU campus. The murder is identical to that of the two other victims. With Mathers behind bars, the question arises: is Mathers innocent, or is a copycat serial killer on the loose?

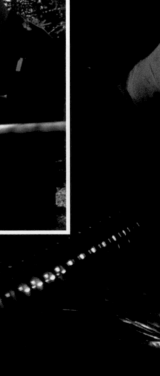

Fly Caught in a Web
The killer would prowl the WLVU campus at night, coating outdoor railings near water fountains. He used blue paint, mixed with motor oil to slow the drying process. He would lie in wait as his prey touched the wet paint, and as she approached the fountain to wash up, he would pounce.

DNA results from the hairs verify Mathers is guilty. Roth's parents ask Catherine to attend the execution. This victory is bittersweet, as evidence confirms Mathers was actually the copycat killer of the two victims before Roth. The real killer will strike again.

EVIDENCE EVIDENCE EVIDE

Dust to Dust

Two years after Mathers is executed, CSI is called back to the WLVU campus. This time, Gil Grissom is investigating maggots feeding on human remains found in a pile of wood chips. The victim is a missing fraternity pledge, last seen by his friends dressed in drag for a "hazing" ritual.

Trace evidence found on a fingernail of the dead frat boy links the case back to the past. Soon after the discovery, a trash bag appears on campus containing the next victim—a female blow up doll.

ELECTROSTATIC DETECTION—IMPRESSION ON PAPER

Using a carbon aerosol and a metal wand to process a note found inside the doll, Grissom finds a disturbing illustration of a victim.

Artistic License

The drawing also features vehicle windows that match a 1983 Chevy van and a neon sign is consistent with that of a local adult store. There CSI finds the van and the body of the latest victim. The shop clerk describes the suspect, who also fancies himself as a comic book artist. Copy ink from his crudely printed books identifies the killer as Kevin Greer, an employee at the WLVU copy store.

Looks Can Kill

Greer turns himself into police, showing no sign of remorse. A search of his home yields locks of hair taken from all of his victims, plus another labeled "Brit Mosscoe." Looking at a pinup calendar, Sara Sidle computes that the name is an anagram of "Miss October."

Painted into a Corner

Greer admits that Mathers was his partner and agrees to take the police to Brit Mosscoe. While Greer is taken to the bathroom, Sara calls to inform Grissom that the victim does not exist. The police rush into the men's room to find that Greer has suffocated himself with a plastic bag, leaving behind a drawing of his own tortured soul under Grissom's gaze.

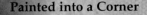

WARRICK BROWN

WARRICK BROWN WAS born on October 10, 1971, in Las Vegas. His father abandoned the family before Warrick had a chance to know him. When Warrick was seven years old, his mother died, leaving him in the care of his grandmother and Aunt Bertha. Socially awkward and bookish, Warrick had a rough childhood, but took his love of math and science to Western Las Vegas University. There, he paid his own way via hard work and a knack for sports betting. Equipped with a Bachelor of Science in chemistry, he joined the CSI team under Gil Grissom, the one authority figure Warrick could admire. His rebellious attitude and brilliant analytical skills are always pulling him in different directions, but Warrick challenges everyone on the CSI team to do their best.

A ROAD LESS TRAVELED

Street savvy Warrick Brown worked his way to CSI via a less conventional route than some of his Ivy League counterparts. Early on in his career, Warrick would often find himself at odds with authority figures, such as his first CSI supervisor, Jim Brass. However, while investigating the case of a hotheaded cop accused of murdering a suspect, Brown and Brass were able to put their friction behind them, and have since been known to call on each other for assistance in times of trouble.

After a brief courtship, Warrick married his girlfriend, Tina, in classic Vegas style at a drive-though wedding chapel. The honeymoon was soon over, however, as jealousy, long work hours, and misunderstandings began to sour the relationship.

Vests worn during scene processing will be bagged after use and examined for any residual evidence.

Angels and Demons

It seems fitting that Warrick's grandmother nicknamed him her "work in progress." Despite professional conflicts that have surfaced with Warrick over the years, his sense of integrity and passion for his work is second to none. Career missteps and vices haunt him, but they have created in him an admirable resilience of character.

Good with Kids

Conscious of his own childhood struggles, CSI Brown has a gift for relating to the young people he often encounters during a case. He has a lighthearted demeanor and never condescends. Consequently, he creates a comfortable environment for children to open up about difficult situations.

After years of friendly flirtation, Warrick and Catherine Willows confronted their mutual attraction, but agreed to keep the relationship a professional one.

"I Can Get a Print Off Air"

Almost any situation can bring out the competitive streak in Warrick Brown. This trait has manifested itself most often as a spirited contest with co-worker Nick. Whether it's over a promotion, a theory on criminal motive, or a football game, both men are known to spar like brothers, always trying to outdo each other. All games aside, when a situation gets serious, Warrick knows that his friend Nick will always be there for him.

The House Always Wins

As a young man in Vegas, Warrick developed a gambling addiction. His habit threatened to ruin his finances, relationships, and career. With the guidance of Grissom, he was able to wake from this nightmare.

Warrick uses ninhydrin in a small fuming chamber to raise a latent fingerprint

Always Vigilant

When an absent Grissom appointed Warrick supervisor for the night, Sara Sidle found it difficult to play "follow the leader." Sara decided to run solo with a lead regarding fake cash found at a murder scene. This ruffled Warrick's feathers when he discovered he had been left out of the loop.

AUDIO/VISUAL ANALYSIS

noun the examination of various audio and visual elements,
including voice and video recordings, to link a suspect to a crime.

AUDIO/VISUAL ANALYSIS

THE CAMERA DOES not lie, and neither does the microphone—at least, most of the time. A person in a city for a day is tracked by dozens of surveillance, security, and other CCTV (closed-circuit television) screens and recordings. Finding the recording is the first hurdle. Some cameras are dummies, simply for show as deterrents. Others are malfunctioning or not hooked up to magnetic tape or hard-disk storage. If the footage is found, the images may be small, grainy, and jerky. But there are many ways to enhance the pictures, and similarly to clarify sound recordings. Electronic filters and computer software can sharpen and recognize a visual or auditory pattern, and pull it out so it stands apart from the background. These systems are fast improving as face-recognition, iris-scan, and voiceprint technology join fingerprints in the forefront of personal identification methods. New electronic passports will ultimately embody all this information, and more, in microchips, which should make identity theft more difficult—until the fraudsters catch up.

Warrick Brown joins specialist A/V technician Archie Johnson to analyze CCTV tape. They study the scenes for background clues like street signs, landmarks, and buses on regular routes.

Lifting the Blur

A surveillance camera in a lift records someone holding a card. Zooming in makes the card fill the frame, but the picture is indistinct and blurred. Image enhancement software looks for tiny patches of the picture that have sudden gradations of "in-between" colors that show edges of shapes. By selecting different colors and enhancing the "slope" of change, the picture comes into focus.

First, the image is panelized. This means that the software reduces the pixelation and brings in smoother gradations.

The image is surveyed for the strongest colors. The way that they compare with the background creates a sharp contrast.

With the image completely enhanced it is clear that the item is a room card key for Tangiers Casino.

SWEET HABIT

Surveillance catches a professional gambler dying, live on camera. The waitress spiked his drink, but this by itself was not fatal. Backtracking through footage shows that he ate huge amounts of chocolate, which had been contaminated in its country of origin.
Low lead levels built up in his system over years. The drink spike was the last straw.

At his studio mixing console, record producer Disco Placid lends the CSI team his expertize and sophisticated audio equipment for voiceprint comparisons.

The Right Wavelength

The latest audio equipment manipulates sounds in any way imaginable. One technique is to localize a voice's main frequencies (pitch), cut out other sounds, and display the results as visible traces or sonograms. The same words or phrases from two recordings can be captured this way and compared visually.

Room with a View

In a snuff video examined by CSIs, the movie-maker panned the camera around an anonymous room. When the team magnify a specific area of the footage they can see the Stratosphere Tower. Using perspective and triangulation, the room used for the movie is pinpointed and Brown confirms the scene with the screen grab from the movie.

Drive-through Alibi

Surveillance at a drive-through is usually to catch robberies or to back up claims of abuse or assault. This visit by a murder suspect is timed at 8:17 a.m. and supports his alibi. He may not have been the killer but he was still involved and details in the footage help to determine that.

TM # 94286
OLY FIELD/
ARYLAND PKWY

04:06:06:17*

8 17 A

Cash Card

An ATM camera records a man withdrawing notes. His shirt logo reveals his workplace—the shop in the background—and leads to his identity. Checks quickly show that it's a stolen card that he is using.

Grissom screens the holding room with dusting powder and his ALS (Alternate Light Source)

Holding On

Cameras are important in enforcement areas such as holding rooms and interview suites. A man who plays at Sam Braun's casino is killed. Reviewing CCTV tapes from the casino holding room supports Braun's claim that the man was alive when he left the room. It also gives Gil Grissom and the team leads on where to look in the room for evidence.

HOLDING ROOM

05-13-04 1:37 PM

A QUIET NIGHT TURNS tragic when a drive-by shooter opens fire on a suburban street. A stray bullet penetrates a nearby home, killing nine-year-old Aimee Phelps while she is asleep in her bed. The crime scene turns out to be in the neighborhood where CSI Warrick Brown grew up. The victim's father, Matt Phelps, is a local hero who made it big in pro football then returned home to run a community recreation center for underprivileged kids. Warrick considers Phelps a role model and close friend. Gil Grissom asks Warrick if he thinks he can handle being on the case, and Warrick insists that he not be reassigned.

The ammunition fired from an automatic gun shattered the glass windows in the Phelps's house. Several of the bullets hit the wall and disintegrated on impact. Grissom realizes the only intact bullet is the one that killed Aimee.

Aimee died almost instantaneously when the projectile severed her spinal column. Dr. Robbins recovers the bullet from where it lodged in her brain stem. The nine-millimeter bullet has splinters in it from the bookcase it traveled through before hitting the little girl.

IT'S IN THE MAIL

Down the street from Matt's house, Warrick and Jim Brass come across a fallen mailbox with a large dent in its side. The dent is relatively high on the box, suggesting that an SUV or van may be responsible for the damage. Warrick spies silver paint transfer marring the mailbox's veneer. The CSIs get a break when a man is caught brandishing an automatic weapon in a bar a few blocks from the Phelps's house.

Warrick and Brass show up at the bar to apprehend the gun. The suspect, Gene Jaycobs, a former classmate of Warrick, claims that he found the weapon. Jaycobs recognizes Warrick when the CSI tests the defiant man's hands for GSR.

The next day, Jaycobs turns up in the hospital, the victim of a severe beating. When Warrick matches a contusion on Jaycob's cheek to a unique football ring worn by Phelps, the CSI is forced to arrest his friend.

Personal Foul

The gun matches the bullet extracted from Aimee's body, but Jaycobs has an alibi and the DA won't press charges, even when evidence surfaces that Jaycobs robbed Phelps a week prior to the shooting. Warrick has to restrain Phelps from attacking Jaycobs, who is then put into protective custody. Warrick obtains the address and pays Jaycobs a visit, vowing to get him for robbery even if he can't make a murder charge stick.

Joy Ride

A silver minivan, stolen from the recreation center where Phelps works, is found abandoned in the desert. Blue paint transfer on the van is a match to the mailbox and the interior is littered with nine-millimeter casings. These findings prove Jaycobs's innocence.

DNA ANALYSIS—LOLLIPOP STICK
A discarded cardboard candy stick found in the back of the van provides the criminal's saliva and a viable DNA sample.

A Hit and a Miss

A fingerprint from the gun helps CSI zero in on Tyrell Constantine, a teenager who Phelps threw out of the Recreation Center for smoking marijuana. Constantine committed the crime as revenge, meaning only to scare Phelps, not to kill anyone.

Shutdown

Warrick admits to Gil that the dangerous combination of circumstantial evidence and heavy emotions clouded his judgment on the case. "But it's not you that's paying for it," Grissom notes as Phelps is taken to jail for beating Jaycobs up. A repentant Warrick visits the Recreation Center that he loved as a child and watches workers board up the facility, hanging "Closed Until Further Notice" signs on the fences surrounding it.

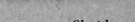

NICK STOKES

NICHOLAS STOKES WAS born into the family of a judge and a lawyer in Dallas, Texas on August 18, 1971. The youngest of seven siblings, Nick stood out through academic and athletic merit. On leaving Texas A&M University he joined the police department, then took a job with the Dallas Crime Lab, specializing in hair and fiber analysis. However, he couldn't shine in the shadow of his parents, no matter how impressive his achievements, so Nick decided to join the Las Vegas Department of Police. In Vegas he found that he could be his own man, and still be part of a high-achieving team.

Tough Love
Nick once fell for Kristy Hopkins, a hooker with a heart of gold. The romance ended when she was found murdered. Nick was the prime suspect until the evidence implicated her pimp.

While still a rookie at CSI in Dallas, Nick discovered his aptitude in the forensic analysis of trace hair and fibers. He could have had an excellent career as a lab tech, but he knew that he belonged in the field.

CULTURE SHOCK

Clean-cut Nick Stokes was initially shocked by the freewheeling culture of Las Vegas when he signed up with the LVPD in 1997. A straight arrow in a city of one-armed bandits, Nick was challenged by the cunning of the Sin City streets. Himself a victim of crimes ranging from grand theft auto to kidnapping, Nick's intelligence and strength of character has seen him through.

Nick has commanding role models in his parents. His father is Texas Supreme Court Justice Roger Stokes. His mother, Jillian, is a prominent lawyer.

Sympathetic Ear
As a man who has experienced crime firsthand, Nick has a special empathy for victims and survivors. He doesn't just see corpses at crime scenes; he sees human beings that deserve compassion. But coming from a family of lawyers, he knows that he must emotionally remain detached to see that justice is done.

Human Nature

In addition to being an accomplished forensic scientist and dedicated crime-fighter, Nick Stokes is known to be an astute observer of the world outside of the lab. His finely tuned instinct for interpreting human behavior has assisted him in solving many baffling cases.

Nick can pick up difficult skills, fast. He's ridden in rodeos, rebuilt engines, and traveled in cranes. He brings this same improvisational skill to crime scene analysis, working through situations that would thwart a less flexible mind.

Nick's patience and attention to detail serves him well as a CSI. Scrutinizing every inch of a suspect's clothing, he is aware that sometimes the smallest or most obscure shred of evidence can crack a case.

Nick had some reservations about relocating to Vegas and starting over as a rookie. But as soon as he had an interview with the LVPD, he knew that this was the lab he wanted to work in and Grissom was the man he wanted to learn from. Early on, Nick felt his competence was questioned by Grissom and struggled to win his approval. Now, everyone is aware that Grissom has no reservations about Nick's skill as a CSI.

Blast from the Past

Only months after his kidnapping, Nick discovered that Grissom had collected the cassette tape from his exhumed grave. Working through his post-traumatic stress from the incident, Nick was able to focus on the audio evidence and, ultimately, solve the mystery of who was the madman's accomplice.

The lab coat protects clothing from chemicals, and helps prevent contamination of evidence

Stokes kept his cool in a confrontation with a man who was stalking him. The mentally ill man had moved into Nick's attic to conduct surveillance on his new obsession and he eventually attempted to kill Nick.

HAIR AND FIBER ANALYSIS

IT MAY LOOK LIKE just a few strands of hair or maybe some textile fibers, but under the microscope, a whole world opens up. Fur or hair from almost every mammal has its own distinctive diameter, flexibility, elasticity, tensile strength, and color. Inside the "scaly" outer surface or cuticle is an outer cortex and inner core-like medulla. This applies to hair or fur from a cat, dog, rabbit, rat, horse—or human. Mammal hair is made from cells that become flattened, filled with the tough protein keratin, and cemented into a long rod shape. The hair shaft grows from a tiny pit in the skin called a follicle. Strands from natural textiles such as cotton, linen, and silk also have their unique characteristics. Artificial fibers tend to be smoother-surfaced and more uniform. All of this information is simply what can be determined from visual appearance, never mind the chemical analysis.

Tacky-coated lengths of gel lifter tape used for prints can also be used to retrieve hairs and fibers. The lift preserves the way the hairs were laid out. Strands lying parallel to each other may indicate a handful of hair pulled from a scalp.

MICRO-VIEW

High-power stereomicroscopes show hairs or fibers in three dimensions, magnifying the sample 50 times or more. This exposes cross-sectional shapes, how cloth strands interweave, and surface features, such as the typical overlapping cuticle scales on mammal hairs. But stereomicroscopes have enlargement limits. A light transmission microscope shows greater close-ups, hundreds of times real size. However, it only has a single lens so depth is lost.

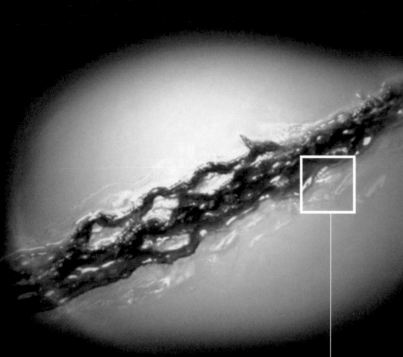

After a burglary, strands of blue denim from the scene are magnified 400 times to reveal traces of cooking grease

Dr. Robbins examines a possible strangulation. Tiny wisps from under the corpse's chin are removed using forceps. Fiber analysis determines that they are from black stockings and the same strands are found on the ceiling light fitting.

Warrick Brown gel lifts rope fibers and hair, plus other traces that may be present. The lift picks up bits and fragments too small to notice at the scene, but which are found later during microscrutiny.

Unravelling the Evidence

Warrick Brown, Catherine Willows, and Sara Sidle have plenty of hair and fiber analysis when a 10-year-old boy is kidnapped and then found dead. Tape-lifts from his sweatshirt reveal long, elastic sisal (hemp) fibers, used to make certain kinds of sacking and rope. There are also dog hairs which, when examined closely, are found to come from different breeds.

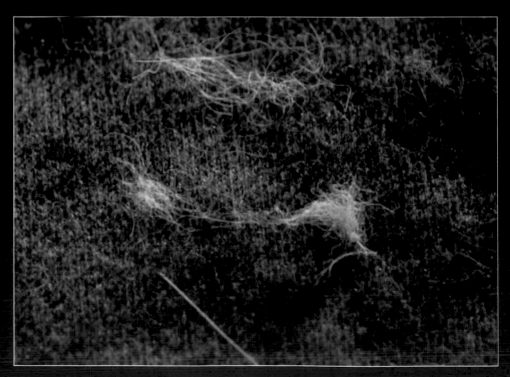

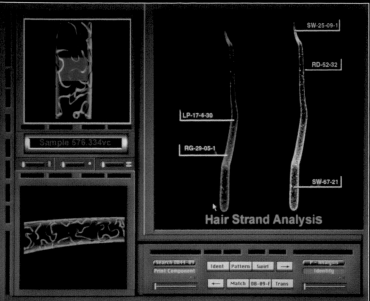

SW-25-09-1

RD-52-32

LP-17-4-30

RG-29-05-1

SW-67-21

Hair Strand Analysis

Sample 576.334vc

Ident | Pattern | Swirl | → | Print Component | Identity
← | Match | DB-89-F | Trans

Small Clue
This human hair is unusually thin and lacks normal pigment in the medulla (core). The tensometer pulls the hair until it snaps—it's weak. These features suggest hypoplasia, a component in certain forms of dwarfism.

Hair Analysis
Computer displays combine the appearance of a whole hair showing kinks and bends with a close-up of its scaly cuticle surface, which is formed from several overlapping layers of keratinized squamous (flattened) cells. A further enlargement determines light transmission through the layers of cuticle, cortex, and central medulla.

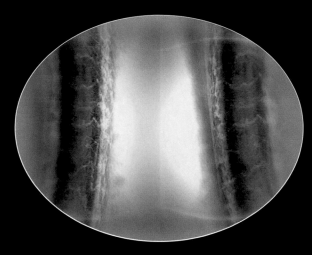

Are two hairs at different locations from the same person? The cuticles are both smooth, the cortexes are not letting light through, which means that the hair has been dyed, and the medullas are regular and continuous. Odds are on a match.

Willows uses a light shone obliquely to cast shadows. This shows up light hairs or fiber strands on a light background

THE ROOT OF THE PROBLEM
Hairs from different parts of the human body are very different. Eyelashes are thicker, eyebrows are thinner, and both taper more rapidly than scalp hair. Body hairs are thinner still and more fragile. Any hair is basically dead, its cells containing mainly keratin. Recovery of DNA is complex and limited. But a hair pulled out by the root may have living cells from the follicle clustered around its base, and these yield DNA more easily.

WILLOWS

POLICE

LV PD CSI

Nick Stokes finds three distinct pools of blood in the foyer and on the stairs. Sara collects toothbrushes and hairbrushes to run DNA comparisons in order to identify who the blood came from.

L AS VEGAS CSI travels for hours to the small town of Pioche, Nevada to investigate the disappearance of Jude and Nina McBride, and their two children, Jeremy, 14, and Cassie, 10. All of their personal effects—cars, cell phones, wallets—are untouched, but the large dry blood pools suggest that the family met a violent end over the weekend. The photographs in their house depict a loving, close family and the local sheriff can't imagine why anyone would harm them. Without any bodies, the major clues that the CSIs have to go on are the messy shoeprints dried in the blood pool. After excluding the family members' shoe sizes from the bloodied prints, Sara Sidle finds a man's size 12 shoeprint that does not belong to the family.

END OF INNOCENCE

Greg Sanders searches the perimeter of the house for evidence. He photographs a tire print in the dirt, noting that the car may have had a hitch attached to it. He also discovers a wrapped piece of bubblegum. Inside the house, Nick senses Cassie's voice speaking to him as he goes through her room. Under her bed, he finds a bottle of cough medicine and a shoe filled with the syrup. In Jeremy's room, Warrick Brown discovers evidence that the boy was selling term papers to other students.

Nick is moved by family photos showing Cassie as a happy, social girl. Cassie and Jeremy played Hansel and Gretel in her school play.

High Life

Sara and Greg discover that the McBrides had a secret: row upon row of marijuana plants line their basement. Several dried plants are missing. Warrick finds two bullets that were used to break the lock on the basement door.

Buzz Kill

Catherine Willows gets a match with a print from the McBride house—a high school junior named Mark Horvatin. When Nick intercepts him at school, Mark is wearing a brand new pair of size 12 sneakers. In Mark's car they find the stolen marijuana and an ATM receipt belonging to fellow student, and Cassie's swim coach, Peter Locke. Peter may be implicated in the disappearances.

AUDIO/VISUAL ANALYSIS—ATM CAMERA
By zooming in on footage from the ATM camera, CSI extrapolates a clear picture of Peter holding a sleeping Cassie in his lap.

Peter has a receipt for boat gas for his parent's boat. Nick creates a search perimeter around the boat's mooring to search for the bodies. He finds the corpses of Jude, Nina, and Jeremy in the water, but the only sign of Cassie is another piece of gum.

Follow the Breadcrumbs
Bullets extracted from the bodies are traced to a gun owned by the father of another student, Luke Daniels. The boys refuse to talk, but Nick searches the shoreline and finds Cassie, unconscious but alive. In her hand is the gum she had been dropping to leave her rescuers a trail.

SOLE SURVIVOR
Nick may have crossed a line by roughing up Peter during the interrogation, but it was worth it to find Cassie alive. Her only injury is a shallow cut across her trachea from when the boys tried, but failed, to kill her. At the hospital, she gives Nick a card that reads, "Thanks for Finding Me."

SARA SIDLE

SARA SIDLE SHOULD have been a flower child. She was born September 16, 1971, in Tamales Bay, California. Her hippie parents ran a bed and breakfast along the Pacific Coast, but the picture of an idyllic life ended there. When her mother killed her drunken, abusive father in self-defense, Sara became a ward of the state. Using her extraordinary intelligence to shield herself against uncertainty, Sara overachieved her way to Harvard, University of California, Berkeley, and then the San Francisco crime lab. During her five years with the San Francisco Police Department, Sidle found her strength in materials and element analysis. Gil Grissom met Sara at one of his seminars, and called on her to fill a rare vacancy on his team, knowing her to be a dedicated investigator with a passion for all aspects of forensics.

Intimate Distance
After six years of working together, Sara's esteem for Grissom has grown into something greater than an awkward crush. Grissom always had reservations about crossing professional boundaries, and Sara resigned herself to the fact that he is a man too heavily guarded to be emotionally available to her. However, over the course of time, Sara and Grissom have become much more than just friends and co-workers.

Crazy Time
While working a case at a mental hospital, Sara's life is threatened by a raving inmate. As Grissom watches helpless from behind a locked door, Sidle manages to escape her attacker, who takes his own life instead.

Grissom once gave Sara a book on entomology as a gift

Metal cans are used to collect evidence for scenes with extreme conditions, such as incidents of fire or explosion

Family Demons
Succumbing to the pressures of life and work, Sara turned to alcohol in order to "unwind." When she was almost arrested for drunk-driving, Grissom intervened, as friend and supervisor, to save Sara's career. After a leave of absence for therapy in a substance abuse program, Sidle returned to work determined to get her life on track.

Getting a Life
Grissom has encouraged Sara to find a life outside her work in order not to become too emotionally involved with her cases. She once defied Grissom's wishes and put her life in jeopardy when she volunteered to act as an FBI decoy in a personal bid to snare a serial killer.

Problem Child

After years of hiding behind work rather than developing life skills, Sara worried she might lack the inner resources to cope with emerging crises. Put on probation for behaving with contempt towards Conrad Ecklie and Catherine Willows, Sara confided in Grissom about her painful childhood.

As a favor to a friend who was paralyzed and whose husband had been killed, Sara delved into a long-cold case. Her loyalty took a turn when new ballistics evidence proved that her friend was not the victim, but the murderer.

TOUGH ON THE OUTSIDE

Under her steely exterior, Sara is a gentle-hearted idealist. She is a lover of animals and nature, but has a difficult time communicating with young people, her own childhood having been cut short. Unafraid to speak her mind, the sometimes hot-tempered Sara has been known to lash out against injustice and incompetence, even if her actions are not professionally savvy. Given her past, it is no surprise that she is openly hostile towards victimizers of women.

Trying to break out of her workaholic mode, Sara began dating Emergency Medical Technician Hank Pettigrew. The romance ended when she found that Hank was already in a relationship.

MATERIALS ANALYSIS
noun The close examination of elements to link a suspect to a crime scene.

MATERIALS AND ELEMENT ANALYSIS

PAINT CHIPS, GLASS SHARDS, plastic flakes, wood splinters, pottery chips, bits of bark or nutshells, scraps of metal—many substances lay witness to crimes and wait to yield their little secrets. Paints, in particular, can be assessed for their color and shininess not only by eye, but by using complex pieces of analytical kit called spectrometers. Some spectrometers, such as the GC/MS (Gas Chromatograph/Mass Spectrometer), also lay bare the element (pure chemical) composition of a sample. As with hair and fiber analysis, various kinds of microscopes are vital lab tools for material evidence. The comparison microscope has a split field of view for side-by-side samples. A microscope's light source can be polarized, which means that all of the light waves undulate in the same direction, such as up and down or side to side, instead of the usual all-angles mixture in normal light. This is useful to show up tiny cracks or to reflect altered hues.

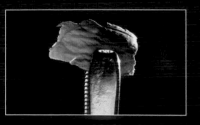

A fragment of peanut shell leads the team to analyze the victim's food. Nut allergies are quite common and can cause severe anaphylactic reactions.

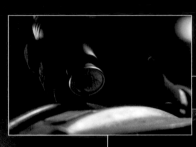

The drum's metal tag is carefully removed and smoothed with a mechanized polisher before magnafluxing. The particles can then slide easily across its surface and find the cracks.

No Longer Invisible

When a body is found in a steel drum, the drum should provide clues. Nick Stokes places the filed down ID strip in a magnaflux device. Oily magnetic particles are squirted onto the strip penetrating the tiniest microcracks. The oil is then wiped off and the serial number is revealed.

Sara Sidle calls a halt to a search as she checks a possible piece of material evidence, having first placed a marker from where she picked it up

All That Glitters

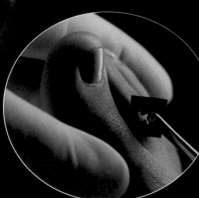

A victim search produces small pieces of glittery plastic from between the toes, with what appear to be "S"-shaped holes on them. Retail outlets can be checked for this, or entertainment venues starting with the letter S—like the Shimmer Club, which is where this came from.

SEARCH PATTERNS

Small bits of evidence must first be found. In a fingertip search, participants proceed on all fours, line abreast, shoulders almost touching. Overalls and gloves prevent contaminating the scene and they also protect searchers who come into contact with hazardous biological material. The overalls are kept afterward as they may pick up evidence, especially at the knees. Bigger areas are searched by walking slowly in a line, participants at arm's length, eyes scanning the ground.

STANDING OUT

A woman is killed at her home. Warrick Brown takes a shoeprint cast near the scene, initially for the shoe size and tread pattern. He notices material from the shoe tread on the cast. This "secondary transfer" material is more noticeable against the uniformly colored cast than it was on the shoe sole. Magnified, it looks like a chunk of fool's gold. In fact, it's a speck of yellow road-marking paint.

A blood-red spot turns out to be paint that matches the door sample from the ex-partner's apartment.

Tough Scrape

Scrapings from this door and the spot on the ring are analyzed using FTIR (Fourier Transform Infrared Spectroscopy). The light that the materials reflect or emit is studied for peaks and troughs and the samples are compared.

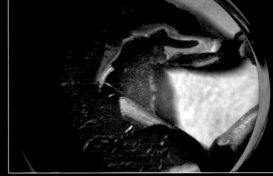

Layer on Layer

Paint databases contain visual and chemical profiles of thousands of paint types and colors for vehicles, buildings, and any other use. The profiles can be elicited from an evidence sample by spectroscopy, such as FTIR and GC/MS. This paint flake shows house paint overlying vehicle paint.

Sands of Time

Sand, mud, and silt are produced by weathering and erosion, as rocks rub and grind into tiny pieces. They can be "profiled" according to their particle makeup. Dark grains in this sample show that one of the parent rocks was obsidian—the "black glass" that forms when certain types of lava cool too rapidly to crystallize.

Most metal detectors employ a wire coil that generates a magnetic field as current flows through it. Circuits monitor the current, which alters when metallic objects enter the field and distort it. For deeper searches, CSI will utilize GPR (ground-penetrating radar).

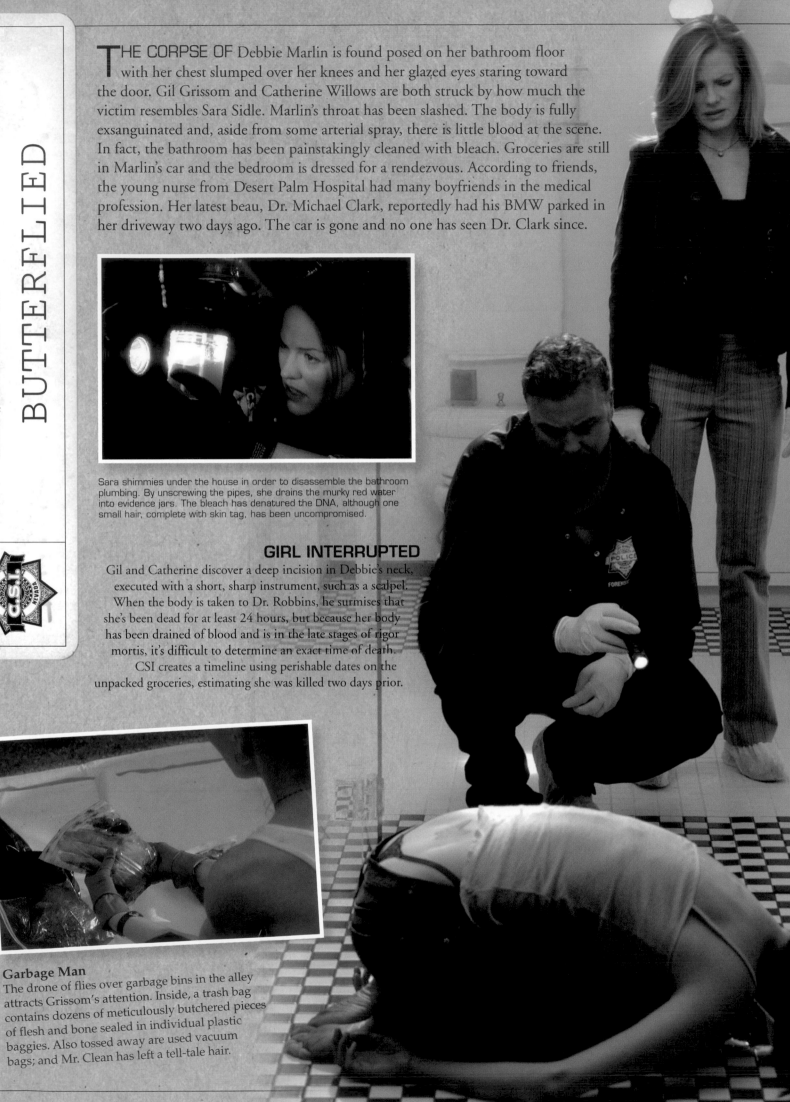

BUTTERFLIED

THE CORPSE OF Debbie Marlin is found posed on her bathroom floor with her chest slumped over her knees and her glazed eyes staring toward the door. Gil Grissom and Catherine Willows are both struck by how much the victim resembles Sara Sidle. Marlin's throat has been slashed. The body is fully exsanguinated and, aside from some arterial spray, there is little blood at the scene. In fact, the bathroom has been painstakingly cleaned with bleach. Groceries are still in Marlin's car and the bedroom is dressed for a rendezvous. According to friends, the young nurse from Desert Palm Hospital had many boyfriends in the medical profession. Her latest beau, Dr. Michael Clark, reportedly had his BMW parked in her driveway two days ago. The car is gone and no one has seen Dr. Clark since.

Sara shimmies under the house in order to disassemble the bathroom plumbing. By unscrewing the pipes, she drains the murky red water into evidence jars. The bleach has denatured the DNA, although one small hair, complete with skin tag, has been uncompromised.

GIRL INTERRUPTED

Gil and Catherine discover a deep incision in Debbie's neck, executed with a short, sharp instrument, such as a scalpel. When the body is taken to Dr. Robbins, he surmises that she's been dead for at least 24 hours, but because her body has been drained of blood and is in the late stages of rigor mortis, it's difficult to determine an exact time of death.

CSI creates a timeline using perishable dates on the unpacked groceries, estimating she was killed two days prior.

Garbage Man
The drone of flies over garbage bins in the alley attracts Grissom's attention. Inside, a trash bag contains dozens of meticulously butchered pieces of flesh and bone sealed in individual plastic baggies. Also tossed away are used vacuum bags; and Mr. Clean has left a tell-tale hair.

After reassembling the flesh and bones, Robbins guesses it would take 12 hours, and a superior knowledge of anatomy, to dismember an adult male with this kind of precision. Prints identify the victim as Debbie Marlin's boyfriend, Dr. Clark.

EVIDENCE   EVIDENCE   EVIDE

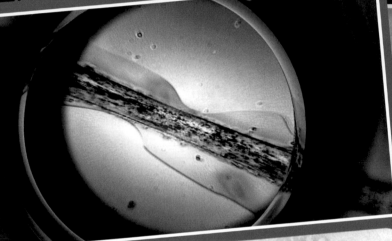

GC/MS—STRAND OF HAIR
The silver hair from the scene is coated with an oily film identified as propylene glycol, commonly used to treat male pattern baldness.

Self-Reflection

Sara visits the morgue to collect prints off Marlin's toes, but she can't help but stare at the familiar face. Catherine is aware of tension between her Gil and Sara and warns Sara that Grissom has become obsessed with this case because of the victim's likeness. Catherine boldly advises her, "The only way you can have him is not to have him. Don't go there, Sara."

House Call

A toe print is pulled off the footboard of Debbie's bed. Gathering her former lovers at the hospital, CSI takes gelatin lifts of their feet. Unfortunately, the matching doctor has an alibi.

Ex Factor

Michael Clark's car is recovered at the airport. Adjustments made to the driver's seat mean that the killer was well under 6' 2". Robbins states that Clark was butchered by a right-handed man. The only right-handed surgeon at Desert Palm, who also uses propylene glycol to prevent baldness, is Dr. Lurie. DNA compares the hair found at the scene to Dr. Lurie and gets a match.

Power Play

Grissom, unaware Sara is listening, draws a parallel between himself and Dr. Lurie by describing the killer as a middle-aged workaholic who becomes obsessed with his young, female co-worker. Grissom concludes that Debbie's rejection rendered Dr. Lurie powerless, resulting in his jealous, homicidal rage.

INSIDE CSI

THE SITE THAT NOW boasts the Las Vegas CSI Headquarters was once a warehouse used as an impound for evidence, particularly confiscated firearms and ammunition. Forensic analysts, working out of back offices of the police department, soon found themselves without space for the new equipment being introduced into the profession. As a result, in the early 1980s, the city council approved plans to expand and update the building. The facility was renovated to include half a dozen laboratories that could grow with the emerging forensic technologies and computerized systems. The new arrangement also took into account the need for additional staff, including 24-hour shifts of investigators, technicians, and administrators.

LVPD

The headquarters of the Las Vegas Police Department is the legal system's gateway for the processing of witnesses, suspects, and criminals. Within these walls, an individual would be interviewed and asked for an official written statement. A CSI may be present to question the suspect about evidence relating to a crime. The CSI may also obtain fingerprints and a DNA sample, either given voluntarily or obtained by a warrant. Legal counsel can be present to ensure their client's rights are not violated.

While awaiting autopsy or transfer to funeral or cremation facility, the cadavers are laid out on rolling tables, or biers. These sealed cabinets are kept at a temperature of approximately 55°F.

The autopsy room is a sterile environment where Dr. Robbins dissects and examines the deceased. During the autopsy, organs will be weighed, sample fluids will be retained, and detailed notes will be recorded.

Colloquially referred to as the "VIP room," it is here that the assistant coroner will wash and prepare a corpse for autopsy.

The smaller of the two interrogation suites at the LVPD is used when two suspects are being interviewed simultaneously. The room also features a one-sided mirror adjacent to a viewing room.

Acting as the hub of communication, the dispatch room connects LVPD to every emergency and every cop in the field.

The larger interrogation room can serve as a "war room" when police officials are mapping out a plan of attack for a "sting" operation.

The central waiting area at LVPD is for those who have come to the station voluntarily. Less intimidating than the interrogation suites, it is a location used for more informal questioning of witnesses.

Captain Brass's office is in the middle of the action, only steps away from the holding area, interrogation rooms, and dispatch units.

Autopsy

A stainless steel gurney with drainage system is the most basic necessity in the autopsy room. Dr. Robbins's "office" is fitted with an adjustable overhead spotlight. The high intensity beam sports a camera that enables the Medical Examiner to zoom in on the body and view the image on an attached monitor.

The Viewing Room

To watch the progress of an interrogation, the light is kept dim on the viewing side of the one-way mirror to hide the audience. For the protection of a witness, this is also done during identification of criminals in a police lineup.

The CSI garage is an ideal space to conduct grand-scale experiments. It has been used for disassembling vehicles, performing blood spatter reenactments, and fuming large objects for fingerprints. The industrial sized fan keeps the room ventilated and free of toxic fumes.

Lab Explosion
An accidental explosion in the DNA lab injured lab tech Greg Sanders and destroyed evidence in dozens of open investigations. Sanders recovered and the lab was rebuilt, but CSI had to work overtime in order to provide new indisputable evidence to be exhibited in court.

The layout room is dominated by a glass light table and is surrounded on all sides by crime scene photos of active cases.

CSI Headquarters
Located near the morgue and down the block from the LVPD station, CSI HQ is centrally positioned so that on-call investigators can easily travel between the labs, an autopsy, and an interrogation at a moment's notice. The building is closed to the public, which helps to keep information secure and the staff focused.

The equipment in the DNA lab replicates, analyzes, and identifies samples of tissues and serums to implicate or exonerate suspects.

The studious supervisor, Gil Grissom, can often be found in his one-of-a-kind office poring over research or mastering a crossword puzzle.

Technicians in the fingerprint lab lift, scan, and run sample prints through computer databases, such as AFIS, to find a match.

The layout room is an ideal location to reassemble or sift through evidence, and also an excellent space for the team to meet and review elements of an investigation.

The ballistics lab is home to an array of sample firearms and ammunition, safely locked away, and used primarily for purpose of comparison.

The décor in Conrad Ecklie's immaculate office is a stark contrast to Grissom's cornucopia of intriguing clutter. Located next to the break room, he can keep track of employee leisure.

Fitted better than most machine shops, the CSI garage is a place to put on protective overalls and get dirty.

Catherine Willows lost several supervisory perks after her voluntary move back to graveyard shift, including her private office. She now shares it with the dayshift management.

In modern times, virtual evidence is just as commonplace as a fiber or a fingerprint. Archie Johnson's A/V lab features the latest in crime solving via computer and audio technology.

Most evidence is found soaked in some type of bodily fluid. The "drying room" is an area to hang items, like a blood-soaked shirt, in preparation for analysis.

Each investigator is assigned a locker where they safeguard personal items, protective uniform garments, a change of clothes, and their essential CSI kits.

The community break room is a place to kick back and have a cup of Greg's gourmet coffee.

GREG SANDERS

NORWEGIAN-DESCENDED Greg Hojem Sanders was born on May 7, 1975, in Santa Gabriel, California. From a very early age, he showed aptitude in the sciences, with a particular flair for chemistry. He excelled as an Eagle Scout, and earned all his badges in record time. Greg was educated in a private school for gifted students and graduated Phi Beta Kappa from Stanford University a year early. After a stint with the San Francisco Police Department, Greg joined the Las Vegas Crime Lab as a DNA technician and was soon yearning to find a place beyond the laboratory conducting fieldwork with the CSI team. Having always been the youngest and geekiest of his peers, Greg embraces pop culture, style, and social trends, wanting to be known as hip, as well as brilliant.

Class Clown
Turning his eccentric nature to his advantage, Greg is a source of levity on a team that deals with the darkest side of human existence. Playful, even in the lab, he has been known to wear evidence on his head!

Crime scenes are first photographed in overall shots then in "one-to-ones": pictures of individual elements in the scene

RAT RACE
Greg resents being called a "lab rat." DNA technician is a coveted position requiring advanced education and superior abilities. At the same time, fieldwork presents an irresistible challenge. Greg traded the lab for the crime scene to test his skills to the limit, bringing scientific precision to the chaos of the outside world—and back again. It is this taste for variety that makes for a genius in the laboratory and a genius in the field.

Fieldwork Crash Course
After years of imagining the adventure of fieldwork, Greg got his chance to try it when a catastrophic bus accident required all hands to work the scene. When faced with his first challenge, he froze up, horrified at the reality.

Greg was raised with overprotective parents who never let him play sports, worried their brilliant boy would be put in harm's way. He has hesitated in telling them about his career change, afraid that they wouldn't approve.

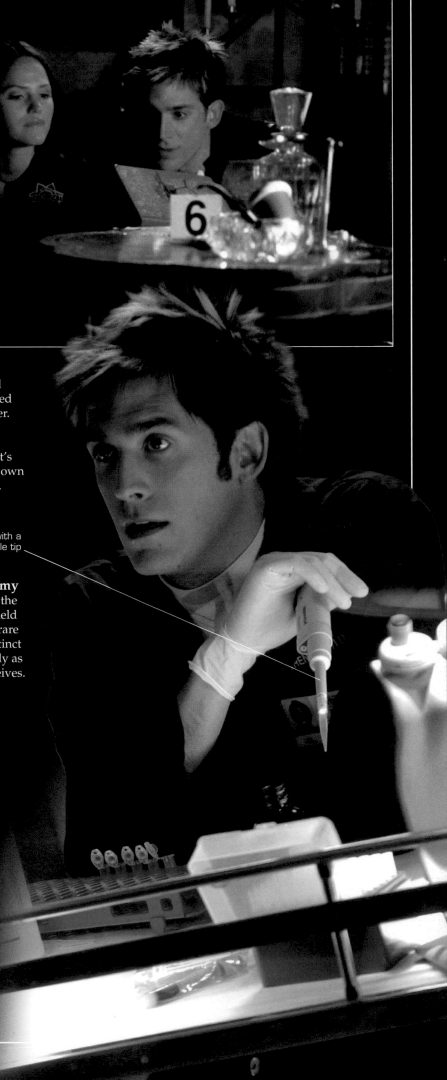

Hidden Talent
Just as committed to his personal and spiritual life, Greg believes he inherited psychic abilities from his grandmother. His sixth sense once told him that he should be dating his co-worker Sara Sidle. Like many of Greg's interests, it's hard to tell if he really believes in his own psychic powers, or is just trying it on.

Greg uses a pipette with a sterile, disposable tip

Alchemy
In the crime detection profession, the career of a DNA lab technician is held in very high regard. But it takes a rare amalgamation of science and instinct to work a scene: the lab is only as good as the evidence it receives.

Greg's field proficiency test yielded mixed results. He found an elusive murder weapon in a toilet tank—but only because he used the toilet, which compromised the crime scene. This unfortunate incident was a blot on his record.

Greg's mettle was tested when he was shot at while working a scene. His hands shook for days afterward—not just as a result of the gunfire, but also because he found the discarded corpse of an infant at the scene.

DNA EVIDENCE

DEOXYRIBONUCLEIC ACID exists in almost every living thing, from microbes to oak trees, worms to whales, and, of course, human beings. This double-helix molecule contains immense twin strings of chemicals called bases, which are like the letters of a chemical code. The letters spell out words for an instruction book that tells the organism how to grow, develop, and maintain itself. Each "word" is a gene—an instruction for making a particular bit of the organism. In a human the complete set of DNA, or genome, consists of about three billion bases (letters), which represents coding for around 28,000 genes. Since every person's DNA is slightly different (apart from identical twins), this substance represents the ultimate in personal evidence—a chemical version of the fingerprint.

Taking a Sample
DNA is sited in the control centre, or nucleus, of nearly every kind of cell in the body. (In a few cell types, like mature red blood cells, it has disintegrated.) A convenient source is cells from the cheek lining, which slough off naturally in millions as we eat. Stroking the inner cheek with a sterile swab gathers the cells in saliva.

Traces Everywhere
Any object that comes into contact with the body is potentially a source of DNA. This ear plug was worn by a person rendered untraceable when passed through a meat-grinder. Wax on the plug provided cells for analysis.

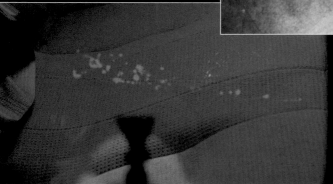

Seat Stain
Most body fluids contain cells and cell fragments from which DNA can be recovered. They include blood, saliva, lymph, urine, and infected pus. In this semen stain from a car, each of the millions of tiny tadpole-like sperm cells contains DNA strands in its rounded headpiece.

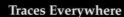

Ribose sugar and phosphate units make up the long coiled "backbone" of DNA

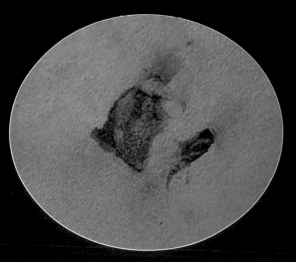

This bloodstain turned out, after DNA profiling, to be a mix of the victim's blood and the murderer's. It was left on a large ice bucket, inside which the victim was dumped.

THE DOUBLE HELIX
Linking the two helixes of DNA are pairs of chemical bases, like cross-rungs of a twisted ladder. There are only four kinds, known by their initial letters of A, T, G, and C. A length or strand of DNA is extremely thin, about two one-millionths of a millimeter in diameter. But its total length is astonishing. A typical human cell contains 23 paired DNA strands, each known as a chromosome. All 46 strands from one cell joined end to end would stretch about 150 centimeters.

DNA Detection

Tiny amounts of DNA can be "amplified" or copied millions of times, to give enough for analysis, by the enzyme-based method of PCR (polymerase chain reaction). The ABI Genetic Analyzer is at the heart of the process. Put simply, the Tech puts in a sample, such as blood or saliva, and out comes an individual's DNA profile. This records the individual trait of how many times brief sets of bases, known as STRs (short tandem repeats), recur along the helix. A sample of DNA can be matched to another, often with the confidence of many millions to one.

Sterile Systems

Much has changed in the DNA lab since scientist Alec Jeffreys pioneered DNA profiling in the mid-1980s. But cleanliness, to prevent contamination with extraneous DNA or enzymes from sweat, is still vital.

Extracting DNA from hair can be awkward, as the keratin-filled dead cells are resistant to dissolving.

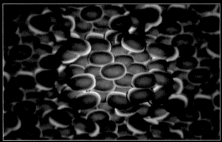

In one method the hairs are treated with various chemicals including detergents, which rupture the cells so that their contents can float freely in solution.

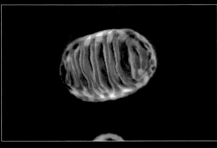

This is an extraction solution to release the mitochondria, which are tiny sausage-shaped parts within a cell that provide energy and which contain small amounts of DNA.

This solution is ultracentrifuged (spun extremely fast) to separate into layers. The DNA fraction (layer) is drawn off and put through the thermocycler for copying by PCR.

Below the Surface

Body tissues that cover or line skin and cavities, as sheet-like layers, are known as epithelial tissues. The skin's surface is made up of dead, keratin-filled, tile-like cells that flake off by the million every minute. Just below are flattened, fast-dividing epithelial cells that resemble fried eggs and are a useful source of DNA.

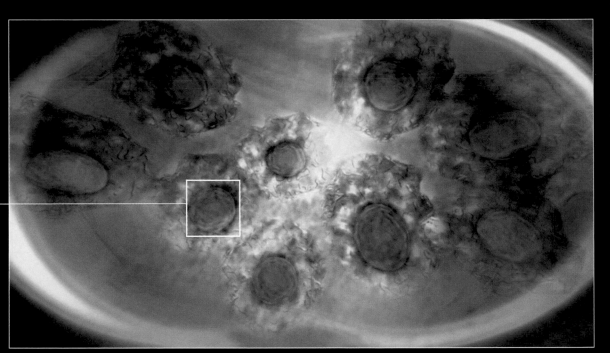

Nucleus (dark central blob) contains DNA

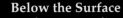

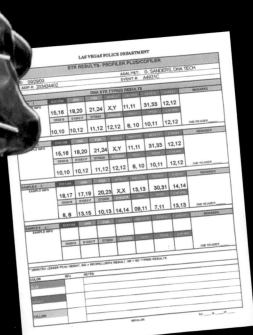

CODIS

The Combined DNA Index System known as CODIS searches the Convicted Offender Index, a database of DNA profiles of guilty offenders, for matches against the Forensic Index, which records DNA information found at scenes.

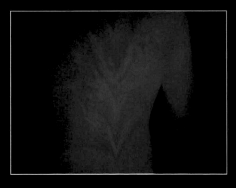

Whose DNA?

Identical twins came originally from the same fertilized egg and have the same DNA. In effect, they are clones. Here, Gil Grissom guesses that a suspect is a chimera—the body is a "mosaic" of two merged fraternal twins, with two sets of DNA.

A 16-YEAR-OLD BOY lies in the street of a rough Las Vegas neighborhood, gunned down by an unknown assailant. Gil Grissom and Sofia Curtis spot four bullet wounds in the victim and 11 casings, suggesting the shooter was firing while on the move. The victim's brother wants to take matters into his own hands, but before he can, he is shot down by a man in the gathered crowd. The CSIs take cover, except for Sofia, who pursues the shooter on foot. In the chaos, Greg Sanders is horrified to discover the body of a small boy in a nearby garbage dumpster. "Our single just turned into a triple," Grissom notes.

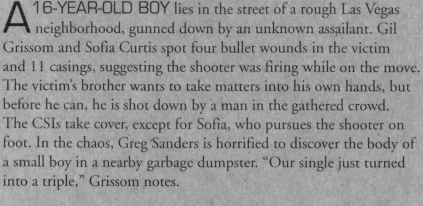

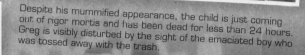

Despite his mummified appearance, the child is just coming out of rigor mortis and has been dead for less than 24 hours. Greg is visibly disturbed by the sight of the emaciated boy who was tossed away with the trash.

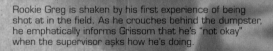

Rookie Greg is shaken by his first experience of being shot at in the field. As he crouches behind the dumpster, he emphatically informs Grissom that he's "not okay" when the supervisor asks how he's doing.

PUT OUT THE TRASH

Greg photographs the boy's rail-thin body as David Phillips examines him. Sara Sidle decides that it is best to leave the corpse in the bin in order to transport him to the lab safely. Meanwhile, the shooter has been apprehended, and Sofia has obtained his gun. When Grissom questions her decision to chase after him when the police officers at the scene were already in pursuit, she tells him she knew the man would toss his weapon aside, giving them the crucial evidence they needed to close the case.

Dr. Robbins determines that the boy was five years old when he died. He suffered from cachexia: his body was breaking down muscle tissue for food. The COD was renal failure caused by starvation. Dr. Robbins also notes several bone fractures, indicating abuse.

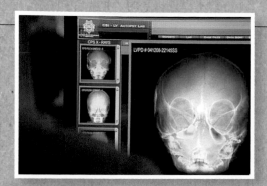

In order to identify the boy, Sara and Dr. Robbins consult X-rays taken in hospitals when abused children have been brought in for medical care. They are able to match the unique sinus cavity shape within the skull to a boy named Devon Malton.

Man on a Mission

With Sofia's help, Greg obtains a fingerprint off the trash bin using the Cyanoacrylate Fuming Chamber. The FBI database produces a match to Private Phillip Riley, who says he took out the trash for a prostitute he was patronizing. He recalls that the woman's name was "Divine."

Greg suspends the trash bin in an airtight chamber, then introduces superglue fumes to raise latent fingerprints.

Unrepentant

Sara and Jim Brass track Divine down at the strip club where she works. Divine is uncooperative but Sara obtains a DNA sample and matches it to hairs found on Devon's body. Divine, also known as Darlene Malton, claims that her cousin Candace took her three kids out of foster care and left them with her, which was too much for her to handle.

DNA—STRANDS OF HAIR
Sara recovers several pieces of synthetic and real hair on Devon's jeans. These are matched to Divine's wig and DNA sample.

Rescue Operation

Divine refuses to tell Brass where the other two children are. Brass, Sara, and Greg search the house but find no trace of the boys until they notice a hurricane door leading to an underground shelter. Brass pulls open the door and enters cautiously with the two CSIs behind him.

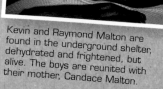

Kevin and Raymond Malton are found in the underground shelter, dehydrated and frightened, but alive. The boys are reunited with their mother, Candace Malton.

TOXICOLOGY

noun a science that deals with poisons and their effect.

TOXICOLOGY

A TOXIN IS A POISONOUS or harmful chemical substance. Even carrot juice can be toxic if you drink too much. But the Toxicology lab usually focuses on substances that can, in relatively small quantities, disrupt metabolism (the body's chemical processes) to poison or kill. Much routine toxicology work is looking for known drugs such as alcohol, heroin, cocaine and crack cocaine, and amphetamines. Another quest is the search for poisons, especially heavy metals such as lead and mercury, and purpose-made agents such as lethal ricin, which is rapidly metabolized or dismantled by the body. These various toxins may be detected almost anywhere, such as in body tissues or biological fluids, in food or drink, or on clothing, floors, and other surfaces.

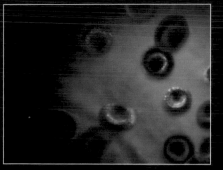

Over the long term, lead accumulates with devastating effects. A tell-tale sign is spots on red blood cells, known as basophilic stippling.

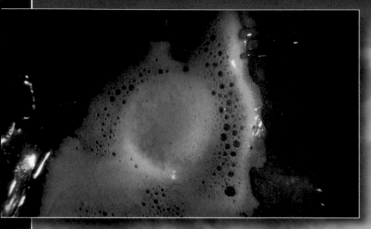

Into the Body

There are many routes for toxins to get into the body, including breathing in toxic vapors, or injecting toxins into a muscle (intramuscular) or directly into a vein (intravenous). The oral route through the mouth leads to the stomach, which contains powerful hydrochloric acid and gastric enzymes. These juices attack substances, like this tablet casing from a victim's stomach.

Spiked Food

Adding poison to food and drink has been popular since ancient Greek and Roman times, when favorites were plant extracts such as hemlock and metals like arsenic. Modern AAA (atomic absorption analysis) shows that this garlic cream cheese contained selenium—a metal usually used to coat photocopier drums. But, in this case, it's from shampoo added to the food in a successful attempt to commit murder.

TOXIN ID

Some toxins can be recognized by appearance. At room temperature, mercury metal is liquid and forms shiny drops. For more anonymous substances, an important device is the GC/MS (Gas Chromatograph/Mass Spectrometer). In GC the substance is vaporized into constituents that pass at different rates through a tube packed with granules, to be detected by sensors at the end. In MS the substance is broken into particles with electrical charges called ions. These pass through a magnetic field and pick up speed according to their mass (weight), giving a wavy-line spectrum that shows the elements present.

Mercury rapidly gathers into shiny, silvery droplets (hence its old name of "quicksilver")

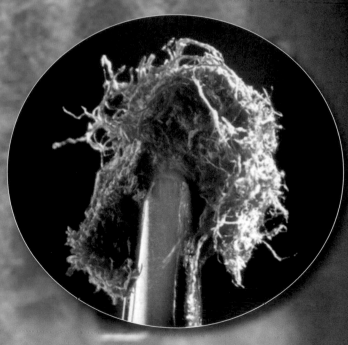

After a boxer dies in the ring, oblique light shows glints on the opponent's red leather boxing glove. A trace substance is checked and identified as mercury. It was injected into the glove for added weight, but also affected the victim with its vapor.

No Pen Pal

Gil Grissom swabs some pens used by a woman found dead in a library. CCTV showed that she had the habit of chewing the pen ends—a possible route for toxin. Analyzing the swabs using ELISA (Enzyme-Linked Immunosorbent Assay) and GC/MS reveals ricin, a plant poison from castor beans. The same is in her body. Apparently she was planning to kill her boss with ricin, but unwittingly spilled some, which got onto her pen.

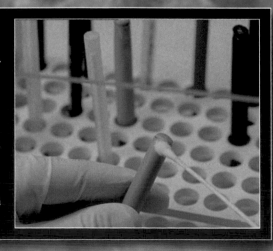

Stain on the Character

Histology is the micro-study of cells and tissues. Histopathology looks at how they go wrong. The skin section (left) is from a man who died at a foam party. Dr. Robbins prepares for microscopy this small sample of skin. It appears to be from a bite on the victim. The sample is first treated using an increasing series of alcohol concentrations to remove its water, then with preserving wax to penetrate and stabilize its cellular structure. Very thin slices or sections are colored with various kinds of stains (dyes) to reveal different features of the tissue.

Robbins puts the skin tissue sample, embedded in its wax block, into a microtome. This machine cuts the sample into slices thin enough for light to pass through.

Puncture Wound

The microscope view of a stained skin section reveals a dart-like puncture area. It has broken into the skin's stained outer dermal surface (stratum corneum) at the top, and jabbed down through the next layers (the lighter stratum lucidum and dark stratum basale) into the skin's main layer, the dermis.

The slices or sections are floated on water. A glass microscope slide dipped under one slice picks it up as a pale flake. It is "flamed" gently over a spirt burner so that the section fuses to the slide.

Snakebite

A postmortem reveals that a victim perhaps bled to death from a stomach ulcer. But blood analysis reveals snake venom, a poison listed on the tox database. Usually it would be inactivated by stomach acid. But the ulcer was a breach in the lining that let the venom enter the bloodstream.

Snakes are "milked" for their venom, which is then used to study toxicological effects and develop antidotes. Close scrutiny of the body did not reveal snake fang puncture marks—evidence that would support the oral route. In fact, a jealous co-worker put milked venom into the victim's coffee.

Mystery Pills

Greg Sanders checks a diazepam bottle with only two pills left. Diazepam is used to treat anxiety and nervousness. Tox tests on a woman who died at a wedding show that she has the right level of the drug in her body to account for the missing tablets—levels that were between therapeutic and toxic.

After more solvents, the section is treated with H&E (Haemotoxylin and Eosin) stain. Haemotoxylin turns parts, such as the cell nucleus and membrane, blue. Eosin makes jelly-like cytoplasm inside cells go pink.

CROW'S FEET

WHEN CATHERINE WILLOWS responds to a call at the Mediterranean Hotel's exclusive Safari Suite, she is surprised to find the scene in quarantine. Dr. Robbins and Assistant Coroner David Phillips, in full protective Hazmat gear, are performing an inspection of the body of a middle-aged woman who appears to have a vicious skin rash. When Phillips first arrived at the scene, he suspected the skin discolorations could be symptomatic of the highly contagious and deadly Ebola virus. Per protocol, Phillips called the Medical Examiner in to check his findings. Robbins determines that the red blotches are not Ebola, but remains perplexed as to cause of death. The deceased, Julie Stern, looks to be well-preserved and otherwise in excellent health. Catherine cannot find any signs of foul play in the hotel suite.

Looking for symptoms of Ebola, Dr. Robbins examines the nasal cavity and eyes and finds no sign of bleeding or blistering. Therefore, the victim is deemed to be free of any hemorrhagic fever virus.

HARD AS NAILS

The autopsy reveals that Julie recently, and frequently, underwent cosmetic surgery. The 42 red blotches covering her body are laser burns from removal of liver spots. Though inflamed, these wounds were not infected or fatal. However, her fingernails have Mee's Lines, white bands of discoloration often indicative of heavy metal poisoning. This abnormality could be explained by toxicology results that detect arsenic in Julie's bloodstream. Most curious, Robbins finds urine in the victim's stomach.

Catherine and Nick Stokes are notified of another victim, Renita Loakes. The 38-year-old has Mee's Lines on her fingernails, urine in her stomach, and evidence of an "acupuncture facial." CSI discover both victims were patients of cosmetic surgeon Dr. Tony Malaga.

To Die For

Both Julie and Renita followed a strict, and expensive, beauty regime consisting of surgical procedures, fad diets, and other anti-aging "miracles," such as ingesting your own urine. One of the potions found in Renita's purse is a homeopathic oral spray containing arsenic. Dr. Malaga, who prescribed the spray, insists that the dosage could not be fatal.

Vials of blood generously donated by CSI Brown

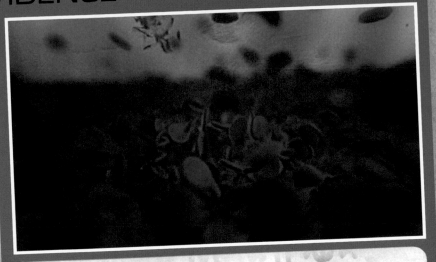

EXPERIMENT—PLASMA
In the experiment, the victim's red blood cells haven't separated. This means the cells have burst causing the hemoglobin to infiltrate the plasma.

Thicker Than Blood
Toxicology concludes that neither Renita nor Julie were killed by arsenic poisoning. However, five days prior, both women had hydrogen peroxide therapy, where a three percent solution of hydrogen peroxide is injected into the bloodstream. The scientifically unsupported treatment, which promises an anti-aging immune boost, was performed at Dr. Malaga's clinic.

Too Much of a Good Thing
Catherine and Nick conduct an experiment to discover what peroxide to blood ratio could cause lysis, where the cells disintigrate and kill a person. By adding increasing amounts of the peroxide to each blood sample, they find that Lysis occurs when the concentration of hydrogen peroxide is 30 percent or greater. The patients were accidentally administered 10 times the treatment dosage.

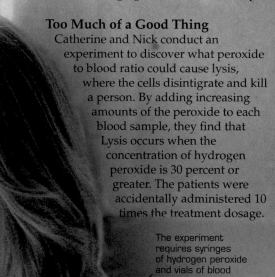

The experiment requires syringes of hydrogen peroxide and vials of blood

Skin Deep
While being questioned by Catherine and Nick in his office, Dr. Magala captures Catherine's image on his computer screen and, without her knowledge, begins manipulating her features to erase signs of aging. The doctor justifies the therapy provided at his private clinic as an important service to women as the two CSIs listen in disgust at his quackery.

Dr. Malaga is unrepentant, dismissing the deaths as unfortunate accidents during elective procedures; something that can be rectified by his insurance company. Unable to press criminal charges, Catherine promises he will have to answer to the victim's families.

DR. ALBERT ROBBINS

ALBERT ROBBINS WAS born on January 19, 1952, in Church Falls, Virginia. A registered nurse, Al's mother brought him up single-handedly, and he all but grew up in the hospital. This early experience with the cycle of healing, life, and death led him to graduate with a Masters Degree in physiology from Johns Hopkins University. While completing his residency, Al was hit head-on by a drunk driver. So began his own cycle of healing. Al spent the next year learning how to live without legs. After 20 years running a low-income clinic and several years as the coroner in Arlington, Virginia, Dr. Robbins took his beloved wife and three children to Las Vegas, where he has since served as Chief Medical Examiner.

LAST RIGHTS

Dr. Robbins believes the dead deserve the same respect offered to living patients. On every victim's body, terrible questions are written; Dr. Robbins finds satisfaction in answering those questions. A childhood among doctors taught him that the greatest triumph is not always bringing health to the living: sometimes, it is bringing truth to the dead.

Field Trip

Three people are gunned down in an apparent drive-by shooting and Dr. Robbins makes a rare "house call" to examine the bodies at the scene. While in the field with his CSI co-workers, Robbins knows to stick to his forte. When asked his opinion of what a scrap of evidence could be, the good doctor replies, "That's your job."

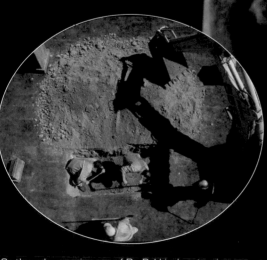

On the sole occasion one of Dr. Robbins's autopsies was brought into question, he oversaw the careful exhumation of the subject's remains. He has delivered hundreds into the world, and cared for the bodies of hundreds who have left it with the same thoughtful consideration.

Keeping an Open Mind

How does a gunshot wound kill a man without revealing an entrance or exit wound? The victim, who had been brawling with his ex-wife, took a bullet up the nostril where it then became lodged in his skull. Robbins indicates the unusual path with a trajectory rod though the brain, as well as extracting the bullet for Ballistics to match to a weapon.

For Dr. Robbins, the more deteriorated a body is, the more interesting it becomes. There are more riddles to be solved in these sorts of cases, and the victory of medical science over the ravages of decay provides a certain grim satisfaction.

The Scenes Inside

For the CSI team, Dr. Robbins is a guide through the wilderness of the human body. He is the only one among them who has scientifically worked with the living, and this gives him unique insight into how processes in life affect outcomes in death. The others on the CSI team know crime scenes with bodies in them. Dr. Robbins knows the crime scenes inside bodies.

Protective garments are always used for autopsies to avoid bio-contamination

On one memorable occasion, Dr. Robbins was given a severed head for examination. This was far from his briefest autopsy, however. That honor went to a severed finger. Much can be learned from little remains.

Scared Straight

Catherine Willows once showed her daughter, Lindsey, the corpse of a murdered girl. Her aim was to shock the rebellious Lindsey out of behavior that could have put her on the slab. For Dr. Robbins, it was a breach of courtesy to the deceased—and, as a loving father, he disapproved of Catherine abruptly ending childhood innocence.

THE AUTOPSY

A POSTMORTEM (literally 'after death') involves general examination of a body, noting features such as bruises and cuts. A major component of the postmortem may be an autopsy, which is much more interventional—dissecting or cutting up the corpse. The basic aim is to discover the cause of death, such as tracing the path of a knife or bullet, or searching for internal hemorrhage (bleeding) characteristic of certain poisons or physical trauma. But the forensic pathologist is always looking for additional evidence such as signs of pre-existing disease or old injuries. The pathologist is usually accompanied by an anatomy technician who prepares and assists, a photographer who records every stage including items lodged in the corpse, perhaps a police officer to take charge of objects removed as possible evidence, and sometimes an independent witness responsible for ensuring fair play.

This bullet is recovered from the body of the daughter of Warrick Brown's former mentor, coach Matt Phelps. It bears splinters of wood impacted to the surface. The splinters match a bullet-pocked bookcase, showing that the bullet went through the case.

A close-up camera and microscope linked to a screen show and record tiny details

The team wear full surgical kit for their own protection and to avoid contaminating the corpse

The standard Y or T incision exposes the chest and abdomen. The ribs are cut through on either side of the breastbone and lifted away for access into the thoracic cavity and the heart, lungs, and major blood vessels.

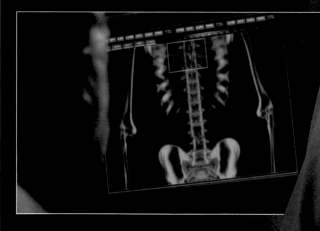

The corpse may be X-rayed or scanned before the autopsy begins. This gives the postmortem examiners inside information about broken bones or items within—perhaps swallowed, or having entered through almost unnoticeable skin wounds.

OUTSIDE, THEN IN

Before the first incision, the autopsy team make a thorough external examination. They note marks of violence, and features such as tattoos and piercings that might help identification. Samples are taken of hair, nails, and fingernail scrapings, and swab samples from the mouth, rectum, genitals, and any other area that could be relevant. As the autopsy proceeds the scene is recorded on video. First attention is given to marks of violence and anything suspicious, especially around the head and face.

Tools of the Trade

The autopsy instruments are fully sterilized after each case, and sometimes before too. Many are similar to the instruments used by surgeons and morticians. The brain knife slices thin samples from any softish organ, not just the brain.

1 Forceps, including toothed and clamping
2 Scalpels
3 Serrated fascia and tissue separator
4 Hook for holding up tendons, ligaments
5 Retractor for holding parts away
6 Brain knife for taking thin samples
7 Long-handled forceps for deep access
8 Bone-cutters for bone, cartilage

Visual Record

A thorough photographic record is taken, focusing on wounds and other trauma, as well as facial and identifying features, and misshapen parts such as broken fingers. Adornments such as necklaces, earrings, bracelets, and piercings are pictured on the body and after removal.

Final Wash

After swabs and smears have been taken, and at intervals during the autopsy, washing clears accumulated blood and other fluids. Catherine Willows and Nick Stokes arrive a little late to request a swab from this victim's ear canal. Luckily David Phillips had started washing at the feet.

Eye for an Eye

The strange find of an eyeball in a bird's nest leads to a woman's part-dismembered body in a landfill site. Was it taken there by a bird known to like shiny bright things? The eyeball is matched up to its face at the postmortem. A perfect fit in the orbit (eye socket) confirms identification.

Gil Grissom withdraws a sample of vitreous, the jelly-like fluid that fills the bulk of the eyeball for toxicological and DNA analysis.

As the body parts are removed one by one, they are weighed whole, and samples taken for later analysis

MARKS OF VIOLENCE

AT THE CRIME SCENE, officers are trained to scrutinize victims of violence urgently for tell-tale marks and signs—from a minor bruise to a gaping wound. The size, shape, and position of the trauma all give clues to the cause, especially when linked to evidence from the surroundings, such as a blunt weapon or hastily discarded blade. Badly injured casualties need immediate first aid, so the CSIs memorize the condition and color of the marks, and try to get a photo, since subsequent treatment and the living body's attempts at self-healing soon bring alterations. With a fresh corpse, the color of bruises and the congealed nature of leaking blood or fluids allow an estimate of time of death—factoring in, of course, ambient conditions such as temperature. Then, after the body is removed for postmortem, detailed study can begin.

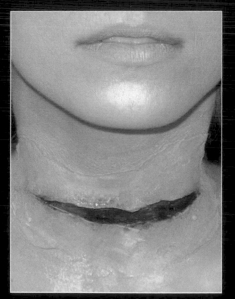

Fatal Cut
Crime can be a cut-throat business—literally. The windpipe and main blood vessels just under the skin make the neck and throat a popular target. Lacerations vary from clean to part-torn to completely shredded. They can indicate the weapon's sharpness, the amount of force used, and how many blows were struck.

In and Out
Wounds from bullet entry (usually neat, round) and exit (messy tears) indicate the type of bullet, the weapon, and its distance when fired. Close range gunshots produce powder burns on the skin. The body part's physical resistance—especially from bone—gives clues to longer-range firing.

The wound angle can show the attacker's handedness (left or right), physical strength, and the height from which stabs came

A STAB AT WHAT HAPPENED
Surface cuts and slices are often tricky to interpret, but stab and other penetrating wounds yield more evidence. Their breaches at the skin's surface are combined with autopsy examination of how deep they penetrate and at what angle. The results may reveal the size of the blade, whether it was single- or double-edged, and from which directions the blows rained in.

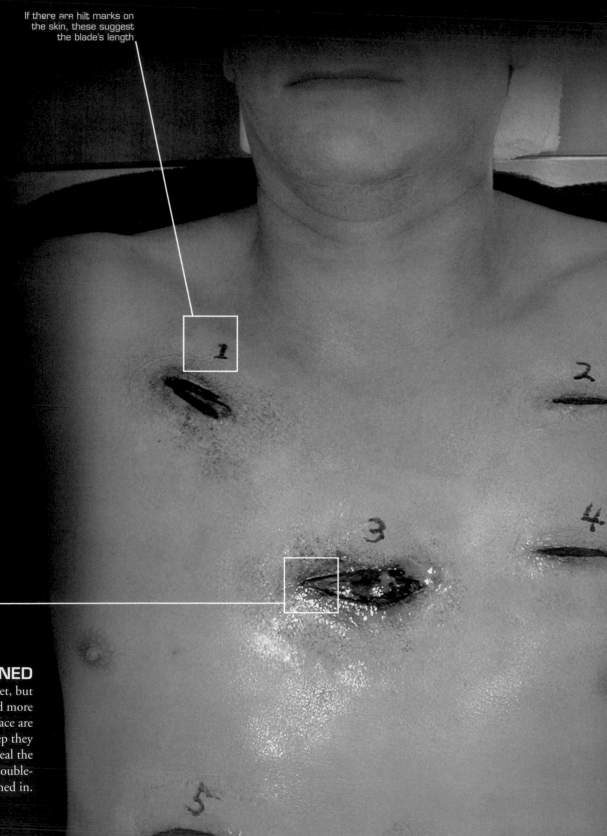

If there are hilt marks on the skin, these suggest the blade's length

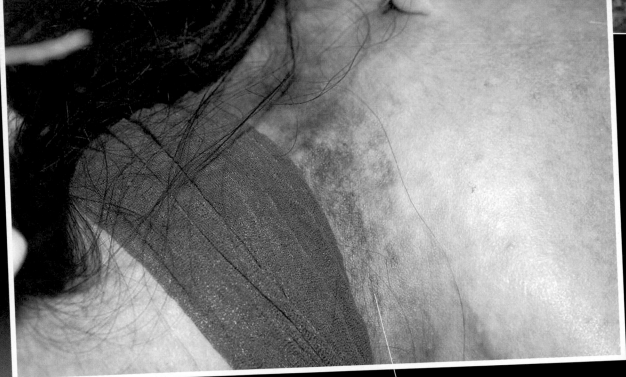

Strangulation

A tightening ligature (cord or rope) or hands around the neck not only constrict the windpipe to disrupt breathing, but also slow or stop blood flow through the major neck vessels, to and from the brain. However, a wide, soft item, such as a scarf, may leave no obvious sign.

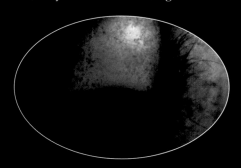

A feature of strangulation or suffocation is petechial hemorrhage or "pinpoint bleeding" in the eyes and face. Small blood vessels just under the surface burst and form red or purple spots, noticeable on the white of the eye.

Ligature thickness can be gauged from the pattern and spread of marks and possibly fiber samples

A Cut Above

Bruises or contusions are bleeding into tissues under the skin after blunt impact. They change color as the leaked blood is broken down and resorbed, from red and purple through brown to brown-green and yellow. However, this occurs at different rates in various individuals and may be obscured by skin color.

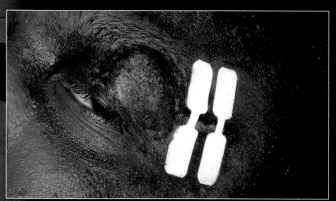

The Hands are Tied

Rope, cord, string, plastic tube, electrical flex, wire, and zip-ties can all part-disable a person by tying hands and feet. Bruising and abrasions (grazes), plus trace fibers or material lodged in the skin, or maybe the teeth, can still indicate the type of tie if it has been removed. Sometimes photography under ALS (alternative light source), such as UV (ultraviolet), reveals latent bruising not obvious to the naked eye.

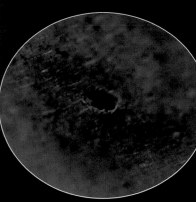

Eye on the Needle

Wounds that are small and round, with well-defined edges, suggest a mark from a needle or pin. Depending on the nature and depth of the damage under the skin, this could be the hollow hypodermic "below skin" needle used to inject from a syringe, or a sewing-type needle that jabbed in a toxin.

Extent of marks signify if the victim has struggled to remove the tie—showing whether he or she was conscious

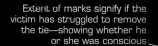

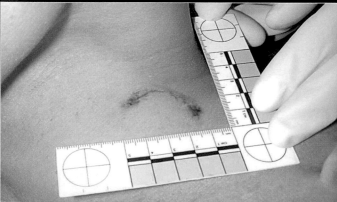

Bite marks are not always perpetrated by the suspect. The victim may bite back in self-defence, especially if their hands are tied. The impressions of the individual teeth and the size and curvature of the jaw can often be matched by dental forensic experts to an individual as evidence of the struggle.

FACIAL RECONSTRUCTION

EVERY HUMAN FACE is unique, even faces of identical twins. People generally have the most amazing memories for faces, being able to recognize one again with a degree of certainty even if it has been glimpsed only fleetingly. Investigators meld these two factors to produce one of forensic science's most powerful and evocative techniques—the facial reconstruction. Like any anatomical restoration, there are limitations. But a suspect's recreated face can spark not just recognition in victims and witnesses. It may also jog memories of the person's facial expressions, and so mood, from which may flow sounds, words, gestures, and actions—all unlocked by the face on the screen. Or the reconstruction may produce a "negative positive" by representing someone whose likeness does not resemble the expected features.

A clean, undamaged skull is the ideal base for reconstruction. The skull of a body found in woodland is boiled to remove tissue fragments and caked debris from flesh-eating insects.

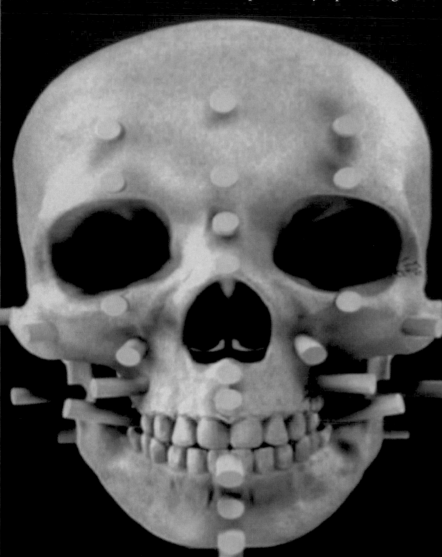

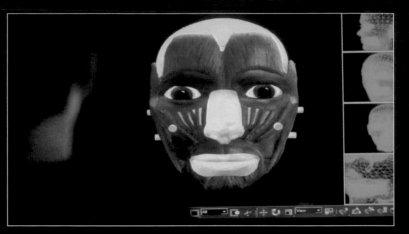

Archie Johnson scans the skull in three dimensions by laser beam and transfers its every detail to a virtual version on screen. The main facial muscles attaching to the skull bones are reconstituted.

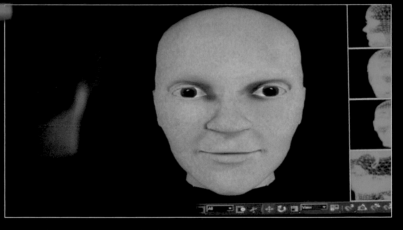

Rules of thumb help to proportion features not represented by bone, such as nasal cartilage. For example, the distance between the inner corners of the eyes is about the same as the lower nose width.

LANDSCAPE OF THE BODY

For more than a century, dedicated anatomists and anthropologists have measured tissue depth—the distance from skin to bone—over 20 to 30 strategic parts of the face and head. Their efforts have led to standard databases for "fleshing out" a skull according to ethnic group. Landmark pegs show a grid of key anatomical sites for this process, such as along the facial midline.

Making Up

Eye color can have a marked effect on our perception of a face. When reconstructing physically, using clay over a skull cast, the eyes can be closed to avoid this effect. Likewise, hair is kept short and simple unless its length, color, and style are known.

This skull's overall proportions indicate possible Scandinavian descent. So, light skin, fair hair, and blue eyes are a reasoned starting point for external appearance, although these can be changed at a keystroke.

Mask of Death

Two women are found encased in tar that had set quickly, forming a mold that contoured their bodies and faces. Sara Sidle and the team are able to remove the solidified tar from around one face and use it to cast a replica—a death mask. It appears that the women were already dead when tar became their sticky black coffin.

The spray-lubricated tar mold is filled with plaster, which sets and is easily removed as a facial cast.

The reconstructed face shape, with its preserved skull bone, shows a previous jaw injury that needed wiring.

A search through files of jaw fracture victims from the suspect's local hospitals leads to a facial match.

LONG-DEAD HEAD

Teri Miller is an expert in forensic anthropology. Her glance at a skull's basic shape and proportions can show its probable ethnic origin and age at death, according to the bone composition and maturity of the wriggly suture joints between the individual skull bones. Healed bone fractures in the skull can be matched back to medical records. Teeth and their wear patterns are also helpful for determining age. Even if the teeth are missing, their socket patterns provide many details.

A Quick Bite

Bite marks and impressions can be matched to a living suspect—or one dead for many years, if the teeth remain intact. For instance, an absence of wisdom teeth suggests a teenager. Even the bite mark alone yields clues. Officers access dental records to support their suspicions.

A PASSER-BY DISCOVERS a long metal toolbox along the side of the road. Inside the makeshift coffin is an infestation of thousands of fire ants who have apparently devoured a human corpse and are using the skeletal remains as a colony. Gil Grissom and Dr. Robbins don protective Hazmat suits to conduct the autopsy inside a plastic tent. When Grissom takes out insecticide to exterminate the swarm, the coroner has to ask the entomologist how he feels about putting the creatures to death. To which Grissom replies, "I view them as martyrs in a scientist's holy war."

Autopsy shows the victim endured multiple fractures, but the deadly blow was caused by two sharp wounds to the back, 18 inches apart. Meanwhile, Nick Stokes discovers a triangular piece of rusted metal in the toolbox and sends it to Trace.

Grissom finds a pupa casing on the corpse and establishes an entomological timeline. The stage of the fly's metamorphosis, combined with the advanced state of the ant colony, leads Grissom to believe time of death to be approximately 19 months prior.

Grissom calls Forensic Anthropologist Teri Miller to assist in identifying the victim through facial reconstruction. While examining the skull, Miller discovers remains of a dung beetle, meaning that the victim was most likely murdered in the vicinity of large animals.

WHO ARE YOU?

Teri Miller completes her facial reconstruction of the John Doe, and lists several distinctive facial features rendered on the sculpted bust, including a wide, flattened skull, disproportionate sized ears and nose in relation to the face, as well as slanted, "epicanthal" folds on the eyes. Miller concludes that the victim had Down's syndrome, a condition where a chromosomal flaw results in impaired learning and physical growth, showing some of the characteristics on the facial reconstruction. A photo of the reconstruction is faxed to every Down's syndrome-related organization in the Las Vegas area in the hope that someone will recognize the victim.

Jim Brass is told that the body has been identified as 25-year-old Randy Traschel of Las Vegas, who was reported missing 17 months ago. The file indicates his last place of employment was the Las Vegas Ranch.

Back at the Ranch

The ranch manager recognizes Traschel as his old mucker in the horse stalls. While interviewing the new mucker, they notice that his spurs are missing a small wheel, which may be a link to the metal fragment found in the toolbox. The mucker says the spurs belonged to professional bronco rider Billy Rattison. A photo of Rattison wearing the spurs at a rodeo in Kansas 19 months earlier implies that Grissom's entomological timeline may be incorrect.

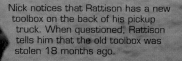

Nick notices that Rattison has a new toolbox on the back of his pickup truck. When questioned, Rattison tells him that the old toolbox was stolen 18 months ago.

TRACE—CARBON STEEL SPUR
To confirm that the metal came from a spur, Nick performs a geometric extrapolation and multiplies the repeating pattern, producing the spur-shape.

Men of Steel

To establish an accurate time of death, Grissom slices layers from the rusty piece of metal in order to measure the rate of oxidation. CSI calculates the depth of the rust in combination with environmental conditions inside the box. They determine that it would take 17 months for the carbon steel to corrode, which puts Rattison in Las Vegas at the time of the murder.

Hot Tempered

A search of Rattison's truck produces the murder weapon: an 18-inch longhorn hood ornament that tests positive for blood. Rattison confesses that, after taking a fall off a bronco and being laughed at by Taschel, he admits to throwing the "retard" up against his truck, impaling him on the horns.

Disgusted by this brutal hate crime driven by ego and intolerance of Taschel's condition, Grissom informs him that "the definition of 'retard' is 'to hold back', something you should have tried."

DAVID PHILLIPS

BORN IN HENDERSON, NEVADA, on June 22, 1972, David Phillips is the son of Colonel Isaac Phillips of the US Air Force. David grew up in the desert towns north of Las Vegas near Nellis Air Force Base. Although he was never interested in following his father's footsteps in the military, he was instilled with a discipline that served him well in both athletics and academics. After a youth spent convinced that he would play professional baseball, David found that his real talent lay in chemistry. Now Assistant Coroner under the inimitable Dr. Albert Robbins, David is thoroughly content in his chosen career.

After the body is photographed, David gets "first touch" to examine the corpse

In the field, David pronounces victims dead on the scene, estimates time and means of death, and gathers the remains for removal to the morgue. He is safe in the knowledge that he provides vital information, helping his CSI co-workers solve numerous crimes.

DEAD RECKONING

David's duties take him from the sterile atmosphere of the morgue into gruesome death scenes. He finds refuge in meticulous fieldwork and is unflappable, regardless of the condition of the corpses. However, he can still find himself disturbed by the evidence of violence found at some scenes. Due to this reminder of the cruelty human beings are capable of, David shares Dr. Robbins's sentiments: "Sometimes I'm glad I only deal with dead people."

Cat Got Your Tongue?
A coroner cannot succumb to human frailty. Phobias, moral objections, and delicate stomachs must be mastered. While collecting the body of a woman partially devoured by her starving housecats, David was almost overcome—not with horror, but with his allergy to cats!

David is an expert in the use of the fluoroscope, a device that shows X-ray images on a fluorescent monitor. He uses it to locate foreign objects buried inside a corpse. The fluoroscope can recover valuable evidence, such as bullets, fragments of glass, surgical implants, needles, and other objects that might otherwise go undetected.

Ladies' Man

For his first few years in the coroner's office working with CSI Las Vegas, David had a schoolboy crush on Sara Sidle, one of the few women he met on the job. Although she rebuffed his awkward advances, she also provided him with a variety of useful tips on how to attract women. This sisterly guidance eventually worked, and David found himself engaged to be married.

Role Model

David feels the utmost respect for the victim when dealing with human remains. But his greatest respect is for his boss and mentor, Dr. Robbins, from whom he learns something new with every assignment. Dr. Robbins appreciates David's careful work, and is confident enough in David's abilities to support his theories and conclusions—although Robbins won't hesitate with a second opinion.

Body of Evidence

When moving a body from the scene to the morgue, David must ensure the integrity of the remains, avoiding contamination by particles or fluids. He must also collect any stray fragments of the corpse, including bits that are dislodged during transport. Any part of a body, no matter how small, can harbor a clue.

CSIs are always on hand to help

Articles found in contact with the corpse must also be collected

Bodies in advanced states of decay must be handled with extreme care

DAVID HODGES

ALWAYS THE TEACHER'S PET, even when pursuing his master's degree in biochemistry, David Hodges was born with an aggressive need to succeed. He paid his dues as a Trace technician at the Los Angeles Crime Lab and was transferred to Las Vegas in 2003. Rumor has it that Hodges's move to Las Vegas was initiated by supervisors at his old job who had personality conflicts with him. While Los Angeles may have had enough of his disrespectful attitude, Hodges believes that his cranky, sarcastic edge is part of his "charm." In Las Vegas, he was sure to mind his manners around his new supervisors, often overcompensating and coming across as a sycophant. Underneath his impertinent exterior is a man who knows himself to be a genius and wants desperately to be appreciated as such.

During a frantic search to rescue Nick Stokes from an early grave, Hodges discovered trace of explosives in the prototype coffin. He averted the disaster by placing an urgent call to the scene and relaying the news.

The Odd Couple
Hodges and Greg Sanders often exchange verbal blows with good humor. Somewhere in his high-school boy brain, the socially awkward Hodges is threatened by the hip and popular Sanders. Therefore, Hodges never misses an opportunity to take a shot at the former DNA tech, be it about his personal hygiene or his inexperience in the field.

Gil Grissom and Sara Sidle catch Hodges in a moment of vanity as he scans his scalp for emerging grey hairs. On another occasion, a reality television show sent a camera crew to film the progress of a case and Sara found Hodges preparing for his "close up."

Hodges admits that he's baffled by a woman's behavior and has turned to Catherine Willows for dating advice. Although he had the impression that he was more than just friends with one lady, Catherine assessed the situation and told him not to get his hopes up.

An explosion in the DNA lab put Hodges in the hot seat when it was discovered that he was handling volatile chemicals in that area before the blast.

You Can Count on Me
Loving to be the center of attention at the lab, nothing gives Hodges more of a thrill than identifying a distinctive piece of trace evidence. A believer that there is power in knowledge, he fancies himself as the one who cracks all of the cases for CSI.

LEGEND IN HIS OWN MIND

For David Hodges there may be no "I" in team, but he can certainly find the "me" in there somewhere. He is what psychologists would consider to be a classic "cerebral narcissist," or someone who derives their self-love from intelligence or academic achievements. Like many narcissists, Hodges is oversensitive when subjected to any criticism, no matter how constructive. His delicate self-esteem has trouble processing how he relates to the world, because he is too self-involved.

Look Down, Kiss Up

While he may have a tendency to fawn over the boss, Hodges doesn't go to the trouble of editing his behavior for those lower in the ranks. More often than not, his rants or ill-timed humor end up being an ineffective nuisance. Apparently immune to the irritation that he inspires in others, he likes to think of this attitude as his work persona; they haven't yet gotten the "full David Hodges experience."

As Hodges became more familiar with his co-workers, he let more of his private life shine through at the lab. For instance, he has been known to bring one of his more unique hobbies into the workplace. He is an aficionado of classic television shows and, in particular, the board games that the kitschy programs are based on.

THE LAB TECHS

WHAT IS THE CSI'S secret weapon for crime solving? The answer has to be the many talented technicians working diligently behind the scenes to process and analyze the evidence collected by their criminalist counterparts. The members of this team are each highly specialized in their own areas of forensics, such as ballistics, fingerprints, DNA, and trace analysis. Many forensic technicians earn advanced college degrees before landing a coveted position at a crime lab. Throughout their careers, they will be called upon by the court system to serve as expert witnesses at trials. Rapid advancements in these fields require them to keep up-to-date with cutting edge technology. Aside from an exceptional knowledge of science, an ideal lab tech will approach their work with creativity, flexibility, and, most importantly, integrity.

Fingerprint technician Jacqui Franco returned to the graveyard shift after wurking days for a while. Jacqui once made a friendly bet with DNA tech Greg Sanders as to who would get results on a case first. Grey won, and Jacqui had to wear a swami's turban for a day.

BOBBY DAWSON

Bobby hails from the heartland of America, where he set out hunting with his father as soon as he was big enough to hold a rifle. Coming from a long line of safety conscious hunters, Dawson was home-schooled in the mechanics of firearms, ammunition, and the devastating impact of carelessness. This hobby bloomed into a career when he pursued physics and criminal science at college. Years later, the small-town boy, to whom CSI Nick Stokes gave the nickname "Country," has made himself an invaluable member of the Las Vegas lab.

Dawson test-fires guns, discharging bullets into a tank of water. By comparing striations of the bullet to one found at a scene, the unique markings can prove which firearm was used in a crime.

The LED flashlight illuminates any inconsistencies, and can catch light and shadows to reveal telling indentations on a document

Ronnie Litra

Ronnie, the eccentric and affable Questionable Documents tech, conducts experiments on evidence involving paper, handwriting analysis, or currency. A smudge of ink can identify a printer used in creating a ransom note and the minute detail in the weave of US legal tender can assist Litra in uncovering a counterfeit scheme. Enthusiastic about his niche, Ronnie enjoys explaining the more obscure and cutting-edge processes, as well as regaling his co-workers with fun facts from his specialty.

Mandy Webster

Fingerprint tech Mandy Webster once had an intimate relationship with CSI Warrick Brown. While the situation caused some tension in the workplace, it did not affect the quality of her work. Because of her exceptional attention to detail, she is trusted with the most sensitive of evidence, including a case where Gil Grissom's fingerprint was planted at a crime scene.

Mia Dickerson

When the lab lost Greg Sanders to the field, the meticulous DNA tech Mia Dickerson stepped in with a whole new assortment of quirks. Diagnosed with a borderline obsessive-compulsive personality, Mia is germ-phobic and therefore wears double gloves while working. She also prefers total silence in her lab. Strikingly attractive with a socially awkward personality, Mia isn't always comfortable in handling advances from her male co-workers.

After several false starts with new DNA techs, Mia Dickerson came to CSI in 2004. While her style may be different, her skill was equal to that of her predecessor and she soon assimilated herself into the team.

Archie Johnson

Eager to assimilate his love of computer technology into a career in crime solving, Archie Johnson came to Las Vegas CSI in 2002. Now the resident audio/visual wizard, he considers the lab his home away from home. In fact, Archie's apartment, which he regards as his private sanctuary, looks almost as well-equipped as his office. Obsessed with electronics and gadgets of all kinds, in his off hours he can be found gaming and writing software.

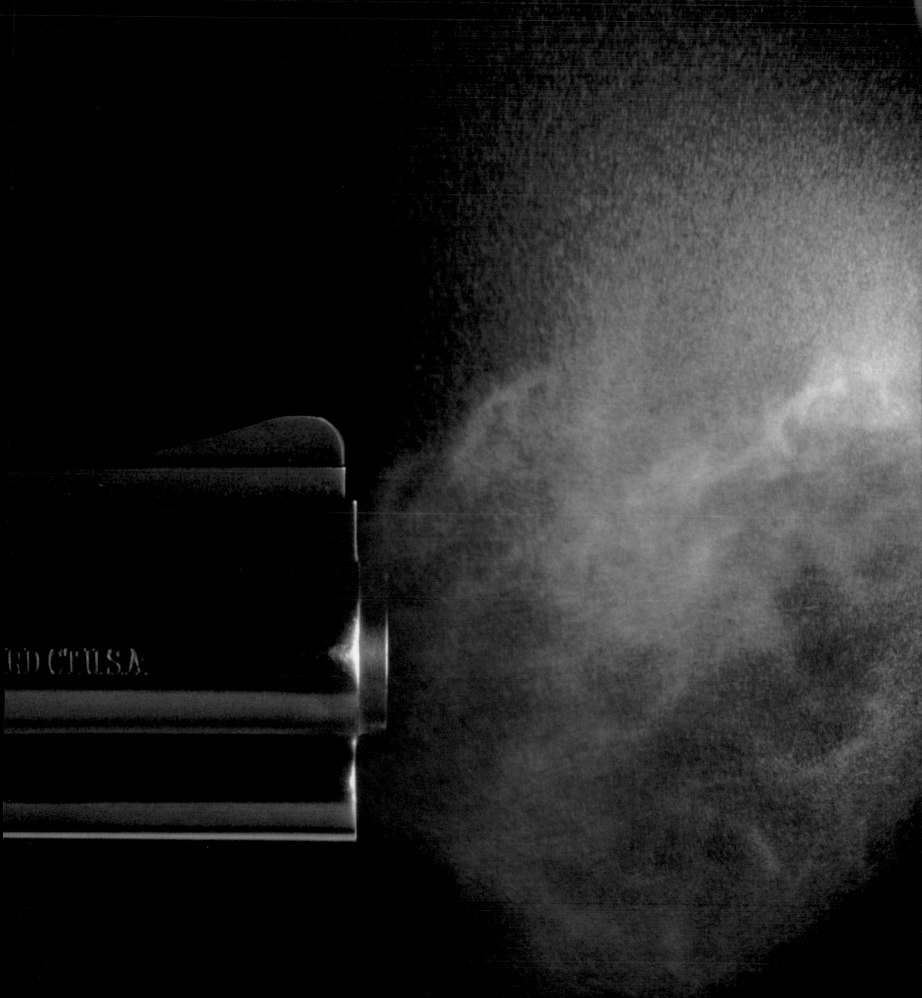

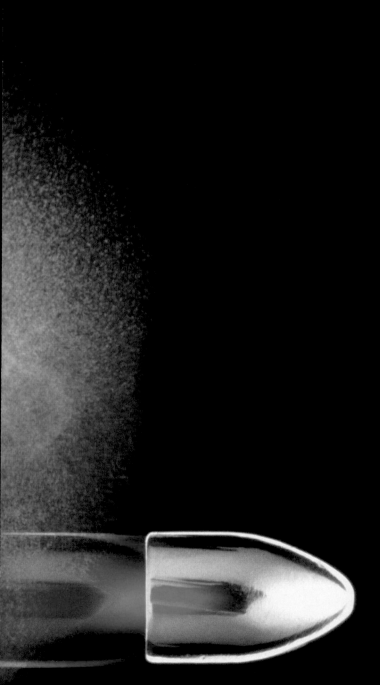

BALLISTICS

noun the study of the processes within a firearm as it is fired; the firing characteristics of a firearm or cartridge.

BALLISTICS

A GUN IS LOADED not only with bullets, but with evidence. It can provide up to a dozen sets of clues: simple fingerprints, material trace, DNA traces on the grip or barrel, powder traces from firing, ejected cartridges, the journey the bullet has made, and marks and traces on the bullet itself. At a firearms crime scene the hunt starts for bullets themselves, marks of their impact, and spent cartridges—the casings from which the bullets explode along the barrel. Cartridges are ejected from each kind of firearm in a typical way and their location can show the shooter's position. In hospital if the victim is still alive—or back at the postmortem lab—the body is examined and X-rayed or scanned to find the depth of any bullets within, and at which angle they penetrated.

A gun from the ballistics reference collection is discharged into the safety of a water tank. As the bullet hurtles along the barrel it receives rifling marks. These can be matched with marks on bullets from the scene or victim, to confirm that this particular make of gun fired them.

RIFLING COMPARED

As a bullet travels along its firearm barrel, corkscrew-like ridges and grooves on the barrel wall, known as rifling, make it spin around to achieve a faster, straighter trajectory. This leaves scratch-like ejector marks on the bullet that can be as recognizable as fingerprints. These rifling striations can link the bullet not only to a type of gun or rifle, but to the individual firearm.

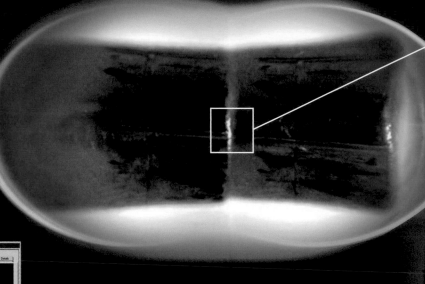

The comparison microscope shows two bullets side by side for direct assessment, here revealing the same rifling pattern

IBIS

The Integrated Ballistics Imaging System (IBIS) is a computerized database that captures images of rifling grooves and lands (flat areas), manufacturer's stamps, code numbers, and other marks on bullets and cartridges. The system automatically compares these to equivalents in the database, to which firearms makers contribute information of their models and variants. The result is possible matches of firearm type to bullet, within varying degrees of certainty.

At the moment a firearm discharges, explosive powder ignites and blasts the bullet from its cartridge. Part-burnt powder residues shoot out through gaps in the casing and mechanism. These can be swabbed from a suspect's skin and clothing, or from surfaces at the scene.

Too Many Bullets?

A routine traffic pull-over turns into a frantic shooting match. The police vehicle has 78 impact sites. Trajectory rods are inserted to show their locations and, where possible, the direction from which the bullets approached. (Similar rods are used in autopsies.) From their pattern, Sara Sidle is puzzled how one officer was shot in the neck. It turns out he was shot after he got out of the car.

Speeding Bullet

In the firearms lab, ballistics gel absorbs impact energy and brings a projectile to rest in a similar way to various tissues of the body, depending on the gel's concentration. Catherine Willows and Nick Stokes test-discharge a gun from the reference collection into the gel from varying distances, using graded amounts of explosive powder in the cartridge. They see how far the bullet penetrates each time to get an idea of the distance from which the victim was shot.

Light on the Matter

Gil Grissom re-enacts a firearms murder. The laser beam shines straight and true, like a bullet's initial path before the slowing effects of air resistance and gravity. The dummy takes the victim's place and the laser angle is adjusted to reveal the firearm's location.

Tell-tale traces and suspicious residues on bullets or cartridges are swabbed and analyzed. They may be picked up as a bullet rebounds or passes through an object such as a window, door, or body.

Trajectory rods can show that a firearm moved while firing a sequence of bullets, as in a drive-by shooting

Some rods show entry and exit holes, giving a more precise site for the firearm

NEVADA
EX C9538

WEAPONS OF CHOICE

VIRTUALLY ANYTHING can be a weapon to wound, maim, or murder. In the CSI archives, guns and knives are joined by screwdrivers, wrenches, saws, and other tools, and heavy blunt objects such as metal piping, chairs, and table legs used for bludgeoning victims. When investigators attend a victim who has suffered a physical attack, they must keep an open mind about the weapon used. Even a large book dropped from a height can kill if it snaps a victim's neck vertebrae. Usually the attacker directs blows to the victim's head, where smaller, narrower weapons may leave marks that are easily matched. The blunter or broader the weapon's striking surface, the less their marks reveal—except when they leave their own traces, such as flaked paint or wood splinters, in the wound. Defensive wounds on the left hand or arm would indicate that the victim tried to fend off a right-handed assailant.

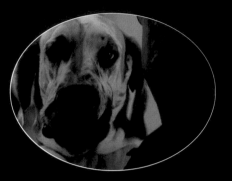

Catherine Willows searches a cinema where a man died from a deep puncture wound to the base of his neck. A bloodstained screwdriver located nearby is an excellent fit. She holds it by the end, to avoid disrupting any fingerprints on the handle.

Trained assassin? No—this dog is an innocent accomplice. His mistress taught him to kill so she could eat the victim's flesh. She believed that it would stave off her blood-formation disease, porphyria.

Dead-Lock
A female inmate is killed in prison. External signs of beating are scanned by a laser beam to translate the skull's detailed topography onto screen, revealing a series of circular indents. A search finds no specific weapon— but the rounded body of a padlock from another inmate's locker matches the marks. Tiny fiber traces on the lock came from the binding the killer used to tie the victim.

The extent of blood coverage on the blade can indicate the maximum wound depth the knife inflicted

A numbered marker is placed to help the CSIs catalog the evidence

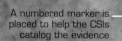

Pigment traces lead to the kitchen where food dyes have been used for a colorful birthday cake

SHARP THINKING
Knives are all too readily available, leading to a high proportion of spontaneous attacks in and around kitchens and workshops. A knife on the floor with half of its blade coated in congealed blood has residues of dye on the handle. If spots of the same blood are found on the floor, this would suggest the knife was thrown into the corner as the attacker ran through the room.

Unintentional Weapons

A storage container reveals a grisly secret—a dirty operating table, makeshift surgical tools from hardware stores and medical suppliers, and a "patient" who bled to death. The body's genital rearrangements point to a male-to-female sex change operation gone wrong. Sexual reassignment procedures should have comprehensive medical approval and legal permission, but here this was circumvented by backstreet "surgery."

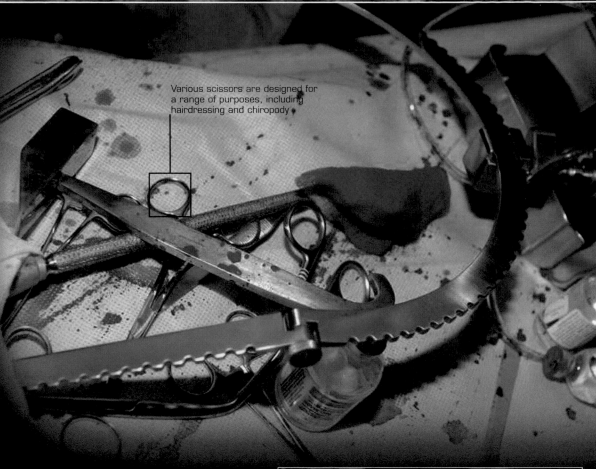

Various scissors are designed for a range of purposes, including hairdressing and chiropody

Certain chemical reagents change color when they contact blood. Luminol glows blue in a certain light, identifying this spade as a murder weapon.

A competitor chokes and dies at a word-game contest. Dr. Robbins removes a letter tile from his windpipe, and more tiles from his stomach. A vicious rival forced him literally to eat his words.

Killer Car

A car bomb nearly kills a woman. Her testimony and the circumstantial evidence make it look like attempted murder by her husband. The officers are unconvinced. In the debris they find the end cap of a pipe bomb. Using solvent vapor, specialized dye, and laser, her fingerprint is revealed.

An indispensable way of opening wine bottles? Yes—and a murderous implement. A movie star has slashed the victim's throat with the jagged point of a firmly-grasped corkscrew.

Remotely Slayed

Robot contests can get heated and even downright nasty, but aren't these machines prevented by protocol from taking human life? Not if they are controlled with homicidal intent. A man's murder points to his 'bot-driving arch-rival as one of the suspects. After swabbing with phenolphthalein reagent, the victim's blood is found on the rival's remote-controller and battery.

DETECTING FRAUD

FORGERY AND FRAUD are popular crimes, especially in the money-making world of Las Vegas. Forgers may simply mimic another's signature or carefully craft replicas of objects ranging from banknotes to works of art. Fraudsters use every trick, lie, and deceit in the book—and the book is continually being expanded and updated. But CSI and lab detective work are hot on their tails. Almost any paper document is full of evidence, from tiny smears of sweat to the types of fibers and chemicals used in its manufacture. The ingredients in the inks or toners, and the tell-tale peculiarities of the particular machine that applied them, such as a blocked micronozzle on an ink-jet printer, can also give the CSI team key information. Even better, handwriting displays a personal combination of letter and number shapes and forms, pressure patterns, document layout, vocabulary, and grammar for exhaustive analysis.

Documents handwritten by the suspect can be evaluated against evidence. In the "London Letters" test a person writes out a passage containing all letters of the alphabet and the numbers 1 to 9, for close letter-by-letter comparison.

COLOR TRICKS

Card sharps (devious players) have an endless array of tricks. One way of marking is a complex pattern on the reverse that, at a glance, looks identical through the pack. In fact it contains subtle variations in line and shape that code for individual cards. High-tech methods include chemicals that are invisible in ordinary light but which show up when viewed through a special optical filter built into spectacles or contact lenses.

A casino player's filtering contact lenses reveal a luminous chemical. The spot's location shows the card's identity.

Fake Theft

A casino hosts Yuri Yamamoto's display of 17th-century Japanese sculptures and weapons but some are stolen. CSI locate one of the swords. When lifting fingerprints from the sword, some paint lifts too—the items are all fakes. And so is their maker, real name Graeme Chen, who produces theater props. The casino's managers employed Chen and arranged the event as part of an insurance scam.

Gil Grissom becomes suspicious when "Mr. Yamomoto" tries to prevent him from taking the alleged samurai sword for lab analysis.

Suspicious Signature

Forging a signature is one of the oldest frauds. The forger can take the original signature and draw firmly over it onto another sheet of paper or a check. The indentation can then be written over in ink. A similar method sees the forger place the signature over the paper or check and pierce small holes, leaving the outline of the signature, which can then be inked in.

Faint ink on a banking receipt can be suspicious

Hidden watermarks, serial numbers, ink composition, and other features make the check genuine

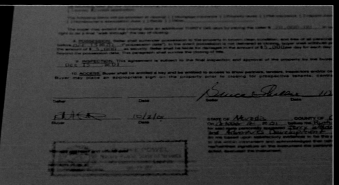

Different Wavelengths

Each type of ink reflects or luminates the full range of light wavelengths in a different way, to produce its own "reflection spectum" under spectroscopic analysis. Viewing documents under a series of narrow wavelength bands of pure color, from red (longest waves) through green (intermediate) to violet (shortest), shows up the illumination characteristics. This ink analysis can be combined with analysis of the writing.

The "disappearance" of different signatures under different wavelengths of light suggest that this document could be a forgery.

Criminal Cash

Inks not only have specific colors and chemical ingredients. They also vary in consistency and the way that they penetrate through different types of paper as they dry. A casino heist leads to the death of a conman. As Sara Sidle documents the banknote serial numbers, tiny oddities in the printing show up under the comparison stereomicroscope.

The green ink used for the forged notes (right) has a different viscosity and spread pattern, and does not "hold" on the numbers as it should.

POLICE

noun the department of government charged with prevention, detection, and prosecution of crimes.

CAPT JIM BRASS

BLUE-COLLAR New Jersey boy James Brass was born in Newark on January 2, 1951. Despite academic promise, Jim found himself on the wrong side of the justice system as a teen—an experience that put him on the path to becoming a lawman. Following a tour in the Marines, and with a Bachelor degree in history from Seton Hall, Jim joined the Newark Homicide Division. After 20 years crusading against systemic corruption inside the force, divorced Jim found himself an outcast at work and moved to Las Vegas. There, he found a home as a homicide detective, and later became supervisor of the Las Vegas Crime Lab.

The LVPD's thick-skinned Captain Brass "can sling scum all day."

Quip Wit

Jim Brass is famous for his ability to wisecrack in any situation. When the CSI team was called on to take the wraps off gruesome Nazi-inspired surgical experiments, Brass's many years of experience at staying calm and detached in the presence of horrific depravity helped to keep his fellow investigators from coming apart.

One case left Jim temporarily speechless: a casino mogul murdered while playing baby in his dungeon nursery. "It takes all kinds" didn't seem sufficient.

JUST THE FACTS

Captain Brass has been demoted, shot, betrayed, and persecuted in his time. His personal life has always taken second place to his professional commitments, and he has paid a high price for it. His daughter was conceived by another man while Jim worked endless overtime. He flatlined twice on the operating table after being gunned down by a hostage-taker, and was almost given up for dead. Yet nothing diverts him from his determination to see justice done, no matter the cost.

Skeleton Crew

Working the nightshift, Jim Brass spends much of his time on the far end of a flashlight. For a man who, at one time, traded sleep for strip joints and bourbon, night work comes easy. Since he curbed his drinking, Jim appreciates the relative peace of the early hours, regardless of the nasty surprises that criminals are always leaving behind for him and the CSI graveyard shift.

After the "friendly fire" shooting of a fellow officer during a gunfight, Brass and Detective Sofia Curtis faced personal anguish and formal investigation. This shared experience caused them to look to each other for strength and support.

While arresting crooked Judge Cohen, Brass recited his version of the charges: "Obstruction of justice, tampering with state evidence, and violating seven articles of scumbag."

Alone Together

Brass and Gil Grissom have something important in common: they're both loners. This creates an odd kind of closeness between them. Brass even gave Grissom power of attorney over his affairs. Consequently, following a shooting, Grissom was able to choose not to pull the plug on the wounded and dying Brass.

A sturdy torch brings to light the evidence that may be hiding in the shadows of a crime scene

Prodigal Daughter

Jim once followed up on a distress call from his estranged daughter, Ellie, only to discover she was working the street. She even solicited him when he pulled up to the sidewalk. He tried to convince her to leave this life behind but to no avail.

Jim realized he had nothing else in this world but his wayward daughter, and pleaded with her to return to him. She told him it was too late. This, of all things, will haunt him forever.

BRASS'S OFFICE

WHEN HE'S NOT on the streets of Las Vegas pounding the pavement, serving up warrants, or clearing crime scenes, you can most likely find Captain James Brass in his office at LVPD headquarters. In contrast to Gil Grissom's den of eccentricities, Brass's office serves as a more conventional pit stop for an active public servant. Adorning the walls and bookcases are a lifetime of memorabilia: a college diploma from Seton Hall, photos and medals from time served in the military, as well as numerous awards for outstanding career highlights on the police force in both New Jersey and Nevada. All of these professional acknowledgements would make any cop proud. However, Brass chooses to keep the evidence of his most important life achievements carefully tucked away in his desk drawer. Among them, a framed photo of his daughter, Ellie, as a young girl.

The Good Cop
Occasionally, Jim Brass will use his office for conducting interviews with people who may be intimidated by the sterile and more formal interrogation rooms. By creating a more personable atmosphere, Brass finds that he is often better able to coax a useful answer out of a nervous witness or a potential suspect.

Wall of Heroes
Outside interrogation rooms at the Las Vegas Police Department are plaques dedicated to the memory of fallen police officers. This wall includes a more recent addition, Detective Cyrus Lockwood, who was gunned down while protecting civilians during a bank heist.

This plaque reads: "Presented to Jim Brass from the City of Las Vegas for outstanding service to the community as a police officer. City of Las Vegas, 1995"

The Cortex
Down the hall from Brass's office is dispatch bullpen. Calls are fielded by the switchboard to determine the type, location, and seriousness of an emergency. Then, the dispatcher will call on the appropriate response team. Dispatch units provide support and backup to the police throughout the course of an event.

CAPT. JAMES BRASS

This plaque reads: "Outstanding Interdepartmental Cooperation with the City of New York Police Department, 1998"

Over Brass's sofa hangs a portrait of his graduating class at the police academy and a vintage "billy club" given to him by his peers on his 15th anniversary of service in Las Vegas.

DOWN TO BRASS TACKS

Far better suited for crime solving than pencil pushing, Brass has always preferred to be in the field rather than sitting behind a desk. There will be, of course, statements to collect and reports to prepare. Supervisors like Captain Jim Brass are constantly trying to fulfill the endless demand for paperwork that keeps the police records updated and the "system" running smooth. After a difficult day on the job, Brass will occasionally dip into his desk drawer, pour an off-the-clock scotch, and commiserate with longtime co-worker and friend Gil Grissom.

One Righteous Lady
On Brass's desk aptly sits a statue of the goddess Themis, a universal symbol of the justice system. The scales represent balance while the sword denotes force. The blindfolded deity is free of any illusions that could influence a fair and lawful decision.

INT[]RROGATION

WHEN INTERVIEWING SUSPE[]TS, everything can have a meaning. Interrogation is partly an audio process where the investigators note not only the basic meaning of answers, but also the choice of words, tone of voice, inflections, pauses, and level of confidence of the speaker. Subtle shifts in body language can also speak volumes. Crossed legs, hand gestures, leaning forward or back, tapping feet—they all have unspoken significance, and can be analyzed in detail by repeat viewing of the interview room's audio/visual records. There are also time-honored techniques, such as separating suspects at the earliest possible moment to minimize their chances of coordinating their stories. In "good cop/bad cop," one interrogator puts on the pressure while the other adopts an amiable approach. The suspect, feeling more relaxed and befriended with the latter, may lower his or her guard and let something slip.

Accepting guilt can release powerful emotions including relief, sorrow, and delayed anguish, as a murderer begins his tearful repentance.

As Gil Grissom questions a woman, she sucks a drink through a straw. Gil realizes he can help the case if he gets the straw, since her saliva provides DNA evidence.

TWO LINES OF QUESTIONING

Catherine Willows and Warrick Brown chat to Bobby Jones after a girl is found dead. A large amount of her blood was drained through puncture wounds in her neck. Jones's demeanor is studied by the CSI team. They have planned to ask him about the same events leading to the murder, but the pair take turns and approach from different angles and degrees of ignorance.

Sucker
The victim was mixed up in a cult of blood-drinkers. During the interview, Jones displays his elongated incisors. The distance between the two tooth points matches the puncture marks in the victim's jugular vein. Jones's saliva is DNA-tested and matches the saliva on the girl's wound.

Mirror window allows officers to watch events all around the room while staying unseen

Decor and furnishings are stark, neutral, and unsympathetic, to produce an intimidatingly detached atmosphere

Room with a View
The interview room often holds two interrogators, the suspect or witness, a legal representative, and perhaps an independent police witness. The interrogators must avoid excessively harsh questioning and monitor the mental state of the interviewee. Colleagues watch events on CCTV. They can time their entrance at a critical stage, perhaps to announce new evidence—and watch the suspect's reaction.

Lies, All Lies
The polygraph or "lie detector" measures physiological reactions such as heart and breathing rates, blood pressure, and electrical skin resistance (a guide to sweatiness). A series of harmless questions establishes a baseline for the suspect, before proper interrogation. But the machine can be beaten and using its results in court is rare.

Minor Problem
Interrogating children and young people is a specialized task needing subtle skills, and which officially demands the presence of parents, guardians, or similar adults to guard against leading questions or bullying. Sara Sidle takes advantage of a casual chat to prize information from a 12-year-old girl.

Special Observer
Sometimes a person observing the interrogation can reveal as much as the suspect under examination. The CSI team allow young Tad to watch through a mirror window as his father claims that Tad committed a murder. Tad's reaction is to give the team information that wraps up the case. He then enters the room to confront his father.

WATCHING CAREFULLY
Brass and Grissom question a suspect in the presence of his lawyer. It's a delicate situation, as the lawyer can advise his client. But simple body language can still show through. A child may cover its mouth when telling lies; in adults, this often reduces to a hand touching the chin.

The rear cover positions of Brass and Curtis prove to be less than ideal during the firefight, as some of their fellow officers were in the line of sight of the gang members.

OFFICERS ADAMS AND BELL, on the job in a working class neighborhood, decide to intervene when they see a man shoving a pregnant woman into a Buick. The cops initiate a traffic stop, but a Chevy Caprice cuts between the vehicles, opening fire on the police with automatic rifles. Captain Brass and Detective Curtis hear officers calling for backup and join the chase. The situation escalates when the Caprice overturns and the four shooters engage police in a vicious firefight on a residential street. The officers shield themselves behind police vehicles and engage in heavy crossfire. Their handguns initially prove to be inadequate defense for the AK-47s used by the perpetrators. Eventually, the automatic rifles run out of ammunition and the shooters must resort to backup revolvers. One man is shot in the thigh, hitting a major artery. Meanwhile, rookie cop Bell takes a bullet to the chest and another to the neck, dying in his partner's arms.

FIRE FLY

The shooters flee, pursued by police on foot. Sofia Curtis shoots a second gunman aiming at an unarmed Officer Davis. Meanwhile, Sergeant Carroll has his gun trained on a suspect, who has his hands in the air. Carroll looks away as Brass approaches, and when he looks back, the suspect is holding a .45. Carroll reacts, shooting and killing the third perpetrator. By the time the smoke has cleared, one cop and three criminals are dead, a bystander is critically wounded, one perpetrator is on the run, and the shattered community wants answers.

Teenager Geraldo Zamesca is found shot in the back. Police surmise that the fourth perp shot Geraldo to steal his bicycle. His father believes that his son was the victim of reckless police behavior.

Under the Gun
Detective Ortega heads the internal investigation of the incident while Catherine Willows collects and examines Brass and Curtis's firearms. Brass and Curtis must weather Ortega's abrasive, and accusatory, line of questioning to articulate their versions of events.

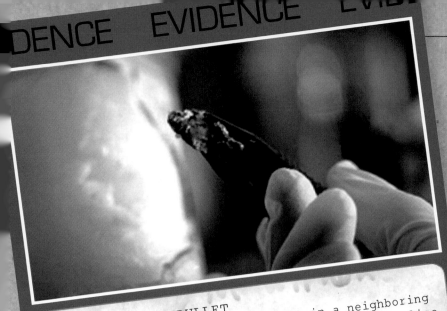

Hitting Home
Dr. Robbins uses a trajectory rod to demonstrate to Gil Grissom how the through-and-through bullet that killed Officer Bell went in under his left ear and exited out below his right ear. The direction of the shooting confirms that Bell was shot by a fellow officer.

BALLISTICS—9MM BULLET
The bullet extracted from a candle in a neighboring apartment has a copper jacket consistent with police ammunition. Blood on the slug matches Bell's DNA.

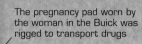

The pregnancy pad worn by the woman in the Buick was rigged to transport drugs

Catherine pulls a fingerprint from the Buick, which yields an address on the driver and his female passenger. While busting the couple, they uncover a cocaine ring where narcotics were express shipped, then muled via the woman's pregnancy prosthetic, to the dealers.

Reality Check
Sofia Curtis and Jim Brass meet at a coffee shop where they feel the accusatory gaze of other cops on them. They are both being driven crazy by waiting for the results from the crime lab. Overwrought, Sofia has been playing the moment over and over in her mind and is now convinced that she fired the deadly bullet.

The Truth Hurts
Ballistics testing is inconclusive, so the CSIs reconstruct Officer Bell's shooting using laser trajectories. First, they recreate the shooting angles of Brass, Curtis, and Bell. Then, Grissom aligns Bell's exit wound with the impact point of the bullet in the candle. The angle reveals that Brass accidentally shot Bell.

Guilt stricken, Brass arrives at Officer Bell's memorial service apprehensive about seeing Mrs. Bell, the officer's pregnant widow. When the two meet, she embraces him and whispers into his ear, "I know it wasn't your fault."

SOFIA CURTIS

Sofia and Gil's first case together was a formal affair when a 419 page (a report of a death) came in during a banquet for Ecklie's promotion.

SOFIA CURTIS NEVER INTENDED to become a Crime Scene Investigator. The daughter of an ambitious police captain, Sofia wanted to follow in her mother's footsteps, but the Sheriff volunteered her for the CSI unit right before she got her detective shield. Sofia's attention to detail made her a natural at forensics work, and she quickly caught the attention of Conrad Ecklie, the day shift supervisor. Sofia was thrown when she was overlooked for promotion and, instead, transferred to Gil Grissom's team on the nightshift. But her dedication and insight soon gained her the respect of her new colleagues.

UNIQUE STYLE

Sofia's CSI style piqued Grissom's curiosity when he noticed that she talked to herself as she processed evidence to help her remember salient details. Grissom even went so far as to try out the technique himself. Sofia takes a hard line: when Ellie Brass was inquiring after her father's pension, Sofia's first impulse was to run the errant girl out of town.

Two of a Kind

Sofia's standing as Ecklie's right-hand woman didn't position her to win any favor from Grissom. However, as they worked together he came to admire her objectivity, honesty, and offbeat nature. The two grew close and have confided in each other in tough times.

After working an agonizing case where a young woman was killed by her stepmother, Sofia decided her time at the CSI lab was done. She approached Grissom in his office to tell him the news, and he suggested they discuss the matter over dinner.

Bite the Bullet

After years as a CSI, Sofia returned to her original dream of becoming a detective and traded in her CSI kit for a gun and shield. Not long after taking the new position Sofia, along with Jim Brass and several other officers, was caught in a shootout where another officer was killed by friendly fire. Initial evidence cast suspicion on both Sofia and Brass, and Sofia turned to Grissom for solace and support. Relief was bittersweet when the evidence proved it was a bullet from Brass's gun that had killed the officer.

Not a Match

Sofia found herself at odds with Sara Sidle after being transferred to the nightshift. Sofia's newfound kinship with Grissom accentuated Sara's growing sense of isolation, which resulted in an undercurrent of tension between the women.

All the Rage

Sofia and Catherine Willows carried out the duty of informing a young woman named Michelle that her fiancé's killer was her own brother. Sofia's intuition told her there must be a reason why Michelle tried to call her fiancé multiple times on the day he was murdered. Sofia displayed her compassion by listening intently as Michelle admitted she was trying to warn her fiancé about her brother's anger over their engagement, only to find it was too late.

Waiting for Sara, Sofia breached protocol by processing a phone booth herself, even though she was not actually a CSI at the time.

Under the Microscope

Ecklie assigned Sofia to oversee an internal investigation when Grissom noticed a new fingerprint on a five-year-old piece of evidence from a murder case. Vowing to be impartial, the two determined that one of the chemicals used on the evidence was known to raise prints over time. Sofia told Ecklie that Gil hadn't violated any procedures when handling the evidence, and had followed lab protocol perfectly.

Ecklie felt betrayed when Sofia supported Gil's methods as a supervisor. Ecklie immediately demoted Sofia and promoted Catherine to swing shift supervisor.

FORMALITIES

DURING A BANQUET celebrating Conrad Ecklie's promotion to Assistant Lab Director, Gil Grissom is paged to a homicide in a lush suite at the Olympia hotel. There, Grissom is joined by dayshift CSI Sofia Curtis where the body of 17-year-old Nikki Jensen is splayed out on the floor in a pool of vomit. They discover a contusion on her neck and a circular impression on her left cheek. Grissom also notes ligature marks and adhesive residue on her wrists. The girl had been attending her high school homecoming dance at the hotel's ballroom that evening. The suite is registered to the hotel's owner, Charlie Macklin, for his daughter Janelle, a fellow student of Nikki Jensen, who is now missing.

Nikki Jensen's liver temperature is 97.2°F, indicating that she's been dead for less than two hours.

PARTY POTTY

All the teens that attended the party have ligature marks on their wrists, but no one is talking. Grissom and Sofia process the suite, discovering a bag of narcotic mushrooms stashed in the toilet. The CSIs identify the drug dealer, Gavin Layne, as one of the party guests. He explains that Jensen had been overindulging in the mushrooms and things were getting a little crazy. He admits to having consensual sex with her, but he swears that he didn't tie her up or kill her.

Buzzing
The surveillance tape shows that two masked men abducted Janelle sometime after they had bound the wrists of the other teens with tape. Nikki Jensen, in a drug-induced paranoia, began to panic. Attempting to stifle her screams, the other partygoers inadvertently smothered her to death.

EAST - VIP ELEVATOR
10:01:43:03

Charlie Macklin refuses to believe his daughter has actually been kidnapped. He is also convinced the ransom demand is just an elaborate scheme by Janelle to get his attention and money.

Virtual Crime
While searching the surveillance room, Catherine Willows finds a handmade device that produces a digital time-delay. To trick the "live" monitor, the gizmo shifts the signal from the camera feed from one elevator into another, almost identical, elevator. Olympia's surveillance technician admits to rigging the switch at the request of Janelle, who was claming to sneak friends in without her father's knowledge.

Crying Wolf

A scrap of a tuxedo belonging to one of the "kidnappers" leads CSI to Dean Tate. He tells authorities that the ruse was choreographed by Janelle and they were just helping her. He reveals that the still-missing Macklin girl has been hiding out in another room at the hotel. When that room is searched, they find it in a shambles and Janelle is nowhere to be found.

TRACE—MERINO WOOL FROM TUXEDO
A black fiber is examined. The texture and diameter indicate a natural sheep's wool commonly used in fine garments.

Suspect Dean Tate takes a polygraph, or "lie detector," test in order to prove he didn't harm Janelle Macklin. After swearing that the kidnapping was just a prank, the results come back confirming that Tate is "Not Deceptive."

Sticky Fingers

A fingerprint found on the room service tray in Janelle's hotel room belongs to hotel busboy, Sean Paland. He admits to being Tate's partner in the faux kidnapping, and to bringing food to Janelle's secret room. While he was in the room, Janelle retrieved a phone message that drove her into a fit of rage, prompting him to exit. The surveillance video and cell phone records support his story.

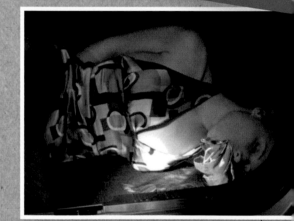

Janelle's luxury car is recovered near the airport. Inside the trunk, Janelle is found dead with a scarf stuffed in her mouth, hands bound, and a cell phone at her side.

Mr. Macklin tells CSI that Janelle had left a message that night claiming to be trapped in the trunk of her car, but he didn't believe her. Autopsy reveals COD to be asphyxia. Catherine studies the crime scene photos and determines that the way the restraints are knotted, she must have tied herself up, but died while waiting for her father to save her.

SUPPORT STAFF

FOR EVERY CSI on the job, there is a nexus of dozens of other specialists, administrators, and law enforcement personnel involved in the process of solving a crime. A patrol cop may be the first on a scene to assess the situation. The cop then calls in the manner of crime into a dispatcher, who alerts the proper departments. A detective will work hand-in-hand with criminalists to process a scene, question witnesses, and review possible suspects. Depending on the nature of a crime, a specialist, such as a forensic psychologist, may be called in to interpret specific information. Upper management exists to provide the police and labs with the support they need to fulfill their duties to the best of their ability.

Detective O'Riley

A longtime fixture with the Las Vegas police, O'Riley retired from the force in 2003. The brawny, no-nonsense cop chose to trust his first impressions when he arrived at the scene of a crime. While he knew his CSI counterparts achieve results with their scientific methods, he had still been known to poke fun at the slower paced "nerd squad."

After 10 years of duty in Las Vegas, Officer David Metcalf is now a fixture working alongside the CSI nightshift. The criminalists rely on him and other "uniforms" to clear the scene and keep the area secure while the crime scene analysts collect and process evidence.

CONRAD ECKLIE

As the Supervisor of Dayshift CSI until 2004, Ecklie was known to lock horns with Gil Grissom. Tension escalated when the politically minded Conrad was promoted to Assistant Lab Director and he was positioned as Grissom's boss. Situations arose where Ecklie's logic would trump intuition and he ended up jumping to conclusions on a case. He would also question Grissom's leadership ability, even going as far as to temporarily split up the nightshift team. However, despite their differences, Grissom still considers Ecklie one of the best CSIs that he knows.

Sheriff Rory Atwater

After succeeding Brian Mobley as Sheriff, Atwater soon found himself at odds with Grissom and he aligned with Ecklie. Atwater has political aspirations so the "go fast, go slow" approach used by Grissom's team often failed to satisfy the media-plagued Sheriff. Under Atwater's charge, a constant application of pressure was placed on the lab to achieve immediate and undisputable results.

When Atwater's goddaughter was murdered, Grissom disproved the erroneous testimony of an entomologist before the killer was freed.

After many years of working gang detail, Detective Samuel Vega transferred back to the homicide unit. His experience with the rough side of Las Vegas and fluency in Spanish have both proved to be valuable assets on many investigations.

Dr. Teri Miller

One of the top Forensic Anthropologists in the US, Teri Miller's reputation preceded her when she met Grissom, who called her in to consult on a case. The instant attraction between the two created sparks around the lab, but the "could-be" romance fizzled when Teri realized Grissom could not separate his career from his personal life.

Sheriff Brian Mobley is a lawman with an eye on being elected mayor. Wanting fast results on a high-profile case, Mobley once made the rash decision of suspending Grissom for disagreeing with the FBI's erroneous judgment.

Detective Tony Vartann

Known for his wry humor and critical mind, Detective Vartann has been working with the CSI nightshift since 2003. Vartann isn't always politically correct, and this sometimes lands him in trouble. But he is a reliable officer with a dual ability for both inductive and deductive reasoning. These are the qualities that initially made Jim Brass believe Vartann would be an excellent fit alongside Grissom's team.

CASE
noun a situation requiring investigation or action (as by the police.)

The women in Lady Heather's employ have been trained to help clients live out their fantasies, whether they want to dominate or to submit.

CASE#02-209-315-615A LADY HEATHER

GIL GRISSOM FIRST MET Lady Heather while he was investigating the death of Mona Taylor, whose naked body was discovered buried in a park sandbox. Mona worked at Lady Heather's Dominion, where the exchange of power and control, rather than sex, comes at a cost. Grissom was immediately taken with the spirited and sharp-minded dominatrix, who proved a worthy verbal sparring partner. When Grissom stated that he considered the services rendered in her abode to be "deviant," she countered with her belief that the very people who shun such a release are the abnormal ones. Lady Heather zeroed in on the enigmatic entomologist, calling out his greatest fear: being known by another person. The CSI was both discomfited and impressed with her perception, recognizing that she, too, was a scientist of sorts.

TEA FOR TWO

A year later, another murder investigation brought Grissom to Lady Heather's door. Two male escorts were killed, and both worked for Lady Heather's internet service. They died from lethal insulin injections. Suspicion fell on two of Lady Heather's clients: Rebecca and Steven McCormick. Steven had hired one of the men to dominate Rebecca; his wife paid the other to meet her privately. Grissom turned to Lady Heather for her insight into the McCormicks, but got more than he bargained for when she noticed him paying close attention to her lips. Grissom let his guard down and confided in Heather about his hearing problems. She understood his fears about the condition affecting his ability to do his job, but reminded him that who he is goes beyond his profession.

During her interrogation, Heather spoke to Grissom through the two-way mirror, calmly stating that Gil knew she was innocent but used the case to push her away.

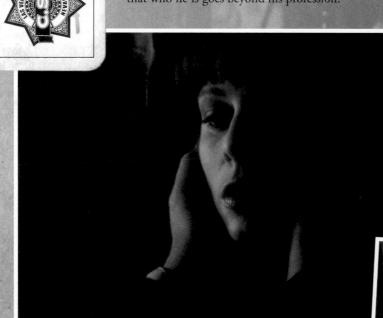

Safe Words

After their heart-to-heart, Grissom spent the night with Lady Heather. Over tea the next morning, he discovered that she used insulin to treat her diabetes. He felt compelled to get a warrant for her needles and insulin, suddenly halting the rapport they had developed. Lady Heather was cleared when the evidence pointed to another woman as the murderer. But the damage between her and Gil was done. Regret drove him to sit outside her house in his car, but he was unable to go inside.

CAPTIVE AUDIENCE

Grissom has never known a woman quite like Lady Heather. She is able to bring him out of his shell in a way no one else can. Heather is the first person he openly discusses his hearing difficulties with. The attraction between the pair is apparent to other members of Grissom's team.

Lady Heather and her daughter were estranged after Zoe, a college student, became pregnant with her married therapist's child. When Heather reported the man, Zoe stopped speaking to her.

Eye for an Eye

The body of a bald, malnourished young woman is found in the desert. One of her hands has been severed, and Dr. Robbins finds that the girl's right eyeball has been cut out and replaced with another. Her arm has been branded with the number 19. But the real shock is the identity of the girl: Zoe Kessler, Lady Heather's daughter.

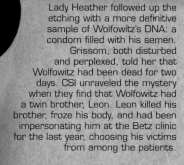

Lady's Choice

Not content to leave the investigation to the police, Heather broke into Jacob Wolfowitz's house. He was the Betz clinic doctor who supervised a medical study Zoe participated in just before she disappeared. He also lived close to where Zoe was found. Lady Heather took an antique etching Wolfowitz had stolen from a book in a library, allowing CSI to test for the presence of the doctor's DNA.

Lady Heather followed up the etching with a more definitive sample of Wolfowitz's DNA: a condom filled with his semen. Grissom, both disturbed and perplexed, told her that Wolfowitz had been dead for two days. CSI unraveled the mystery when they find that Wolfowitz had a twin brother, Leon. Leon killed his brother, froze his body, and had been impersonating him at the Betz clinic for the last year, choosing his victims from among the patients.

Blood Lust

The CSIs discover a lab of horrors in Leon's remote house. There they find victims branded 20 and 21, identical twins sewn together by the sadistic doctor. His work is a gruesome homage to the Nazi scientist, Dr. Josef Mengele, who experimented on prisoners at Auschwitz. Grissom spots Lady Heather's crucifix on the floor and drives to the desert site where Zoe's body was found. There, he sees Lady Heather whipping her daughter's murderer. Grissom pleads with her to stop and seizes her whip. Drained and grief stricken, Heather breaks down in Grissom's arms.

FRIDAY NIGHT AND AN EXTRAVAGANT PARTY is in full swing at the house of former Police Chief Rittle, now a successful security consultant. The scene is far less festive when the housekeeper arrives on Monday morning to find Rittle's corpse in the dining room and no sign of his wife Mina or young daughter, Sasha. The Rittle's car is missing, and the security guard at the gate tells Gil Grissom that he saw a man, who he assumed to be Chief Rittle, wearing a LVPD baseball cap and sunglasses, driving away with Mina and Sasha just after 5 a.m. on the day after the party. The car is found abandoned in a hotel parking garage. In the trunk is a corpse, along with Rittle's LVPD baseball cap.

Chief Rittle is discovered bound with handcuffs, an apple stuffed in his mouth. The anti-cop message is clear to Grissom: "Kill the pig."

CROSSING THE LINE

A little girl matching Sasha Rittle's description has been sighted in Florida. Catherine Willows and Warrick Brown follow the case to Miami. Horatio Caine of Miami's CSI is leading the search for Sasha on a Miami access road where a motorist claims to have seen her. Named after the author Horatio Alger, Caine is a thoughtful, soft-spoken redhead who operates as much on his instincts as he does on the evidence.

Horatio spots a pink barrette and finds the frightened Sasha in a clearing off the road. He speaks soothingly to the little girl, reassuring her that the good guys are here, and they can wait to be found together.

Underwater Discovery

Catherine and Warrick join Horatio at the bank of a canal where a disturbance has been spotted in the water. CSI and expert diver Eric Delko recovers a car with the body of Mina Rittle inside.

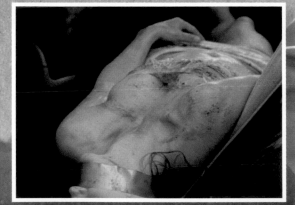

End of the Line

The car is pulled from the canal and Mina's body is sent to Miami coroner Alexx Woods. Alexx finds water in Mina's lungs, indicating she was alive when the car was submerged.

Sex and Candy

Alexx finds expensive tupelo honey on Mina's body. Horatio takes Catherine to a club where the honey is eaten off the bodies of beautiful women. A limo driver named Gordon Daimler recently purchased a bottle of the nectar for a client from Las Vegas. Grissom interviews a woman who dated Daimler. She recalls that he emitted a sickly sweet odor.

Gordon Daimler is diabetic. At the estate of his latest clients, the Corwins, CSI finds blood in the garage and honey on the walls of the shower. The Corwins's boat is missing.

EVIDENCE   EVIDENCE   EVIDE

PHYSIOLOGY—DIABETIC KETOACIDOSIS
The odor in the cap found in the trunk smells like Daimler. His body can't process sugars and converts glucose into ketones, excreting a sweet stench.

Grounded for Life

Daimler is about to take off for Monaco when Horatio and Catherine storm his plane. Horatio informs the smug killer that he has left a witness alive and the crime spree is over. Catherine and Warrick return to Las Vegas, while Horatio comforts the orphaned Sasha Rittle.

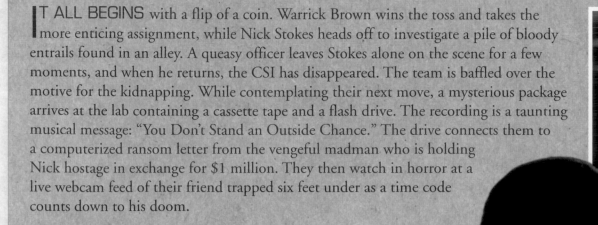

IT ALL BEGINS with a flip of a coin. Warrick Brown wins the toss and takes the more enticing assignment, while Nick Stokes heads off to investigate a pile of bloody entrails found in an alley. A queasy officer leaves Stokes alone on the scene for a few moments, and when he returns, the CSI has disappeared. The team is baffled over the motive for the kidnapping. While contemplating their next move, a mysterious package arrives at the lab containing a cassette tape and a flash drive. The recording is a taunting musical message: "You Don't Stand an Outside Chance." The drive connects them to a computerized ransom letter from the vengeful madman who is holding Nick hostage in exchange for $1 million. They then watch in horror at a live webcam feed of their friend trapped six feet under as a time code counts down to his doom.

Nick begins to process the crime scene, taking photographs of the pile of organs. A peculiar evidence bag catches his eye, luring him further into a carefully laid trap.

The evidence bag containing a Styrofoam cup is found at the scene of Nick's abduction. Catherine Willows and Gil Grissom know at once that this was not a piece of evidence collected by Nick due to the color of the tape and the absence of his initials on the seal. They realise that Nick has been kidnapped.

Trace reveals that the kidnapper used a volatile chemical compound, ether, to render Nick unconscious

UNITING FORCES

Having received the ransom message and watched the webcam feed of Nick underground, Gil and Catherine are informed that the LVPD cannot provide the ransom money. They meet with Nick's parents, who have been brainstorming ways to scrape the money together in a matter of hours. Calculating that Nick only has a finite amount of oxygen remaining, time is not on their side. Even Conrad Ecklie has put his "by the book" attitude aside and reunited the dayshift and the graveyard shift in an effort to recover Stokes.

Nick regains consciousness and discovers that he has been left a few provisions: a gun and a cassette recorder with a brief message from his captor and space on the cassette for Nick to capture his last words.

126

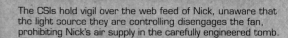

The CSIs hold vigil over the web feed of Nick, unaware that the light source they are controlling disengages the fan, prohibiting Nick's air supply in the carefully engineered tomb.

PLANTED EVIDENCE
The significance of the planted cup becomes clear when reviewing Kelly Gordon's file. She was convicted based on her DNA found on a similar cup.

Prints off a severed finger collected from the corpse of the kidnapper is identified as former aerospace engineer, Walter Gordon. DNA results indicate a parental match to Kelly Gordon, who is serving a five-year prison sentence for being an accessory to murder. Her father has obviously taken justice into his own hands. Jim Brass and Sara Sidle interview the incarcerated Kelly, who knows nothing of her father's plan, but is completely unsympathetic to Nick's plight.

"Welcome to my World"
Armed with $1 million, procured by Catherine and donated by Sam Braun, Grissom meets Nick's kidnapper in an abandoned warehouse. He explains to Grissom how his daughter was robbed of her freedom by the injustice of a legal technicality provided to the courts by CSI. He exposes to Gil his vest made of explosives and presses the detonator, taking with him their only hope of learning of Nick's whereabouts.

Nick uses his firearm to destroy the light and restore the fan. The discharge has fractured the coffin walls, resulting in an influx of carnivorous fire ants. Grissom is able to identify the species, which can only live in vegetation-rich areas.

Nick of Time
Merging the collected evidence leads the team to pinpoint Nick's location at a nearby plant nursery. The team digs up their friend, near-dead and covered in ant bites. On the verge of being rescued, a call comes in from the lab warning of an explosive device on the coffin. Grissom devises a plan that delays the detonator until Nick is pulled safely from the blast.

IT'S 5.15 A.M. when Detective Sofia Curtis is called to the scene of a brutal sexual assault at the Omni Condominiums. A young woman named Christina Hollis was drugged and raped in her high-rise apartment. Hysterical and incoherent, the victim is taken to the hospital as CSI arrives to process the scene. Earlier in the evening, a fire alarm was pulled in the same building but the fire department discovered only a smoke bomb made out of a soda can. A false alarm with a similar smoke bomb was reported a few weeks ago in another apartment building. CSI surmises that the rapist could have been using the alarm to create a diversion to lure his victims out of their apartments. Hoping to have gotten the criminal on video, CSI sends the security surveillance to the Audio/Visual lab for analysis.

When CSI arrives at the Omni Condos they find some unwelcome guests. A film crew from a sensationalizing police-reality show, *Hard Crime*, has been given permission by the mayor's office to follow the team around on a case.

Christina Hollis runs terrified from her apartment. At the hospital, toxicology results yield the presence of a hypnotic sedative. When interviewed by Curtis, Hollis remembers only one thing about the attack: the man paid a lot of attention to her feet.

BEDFELLOWS

Romantic music, candles, flowers ... and duct tape. It appears to be a date gone horribly wrong. The apartment shows no sign of forced entry. The bed is stained with biological trace and bloody duct tape restraints are lashed around the headboard. The rapist's fingerprints are found on the tape, implying that he is unconcerned with getting caught. However, the prints fail to get a hit in the system.

Red nail polish and cuticle skin from the victim's pedicured toes are found next to the bed

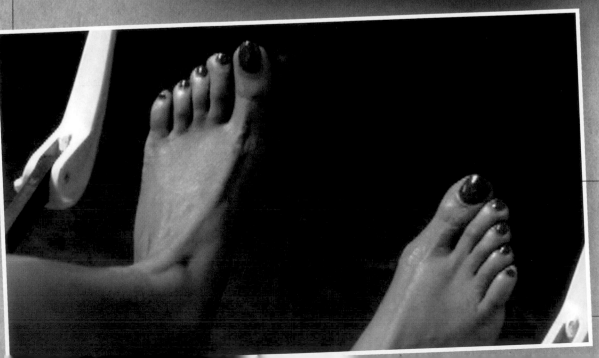

Red Herring

A foot fetish is a visual pathology: the fetishist becomes aroused when close to the object of his desire. Therefore, he would need to be close to the victim to see her feet. The CSI team must work out where he had the chance to become obsessed with a woman's feet before planning his attack.

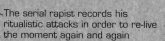

TRACE—FLUORESCENT REFLECTIVE LENSES
Yellow flakes found in the vic's apartment are a heat resistant polymer (plastic material) produced exclusively for firefigher uniforms.

Fire Starter
Surveillance footage shows that a "fireman" entered the building 20 minutes before the alarm was activated. The reflective strips on his coat do not match local fire department issue and the oxygen tank is upside down. Greg Sanders suggests that the rapist carries nitrous oxide to render his victims unconscious.

Close Range
Surmising that their perp may have initiated his crime spree close to home, CSI cross-references their database with residents at the building of another victim, Tara Weathers. The search yields one—Richard McQueen—who has recently bought nitrous oxide. Inside his apartment they discover a fireman's rig and pedicure supplies. They watch in disgust as the video camera plays back his methodical crime.

Catherine Willows and Jim Brass interview Tara Weathers. A month ago, she reported being drugged in a bar and awaking in her apartment physically unharmed, but with her toenails freshly painted. The severity of the serial crimes is escalating rapidly.

The serial rapist records his ritualistic attacks in order to re-live the moment again and again

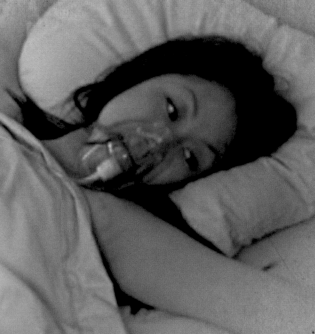

Extinguished
CSI arrives at the site of another false fire alarm to find the real Las Vegas firefighters giving McQueen a beating and a lifeless young woman bound to her bed with a gas mask still over her mouth.

Toe Tagged
McQueen confesses his crimes to authorities and explains the impetus for his fetish. His mother was a prostitute and he used to hide under the bed while she worked, watching her perfect feet dangle off the bed. His reasoning for murdering his last victim: "She wouldn't let me touch her feet."

OFFICER DOWN

JANICE CUTLER LIES DEAD on the living room floor of her suburban house. A single bullet ended her life, shot directly into her mouth by her killer. High velocity blood spatter covers the walls and a wedding picture of Janice and her husband, Willie. The lack of disturbance to the house, and the proximity of the assailant to the victim, leads CSI to believe that this was a domestic dispute. Jim Brass decides to put a broadcast out for Willie Cutler's car. Warrick Brown locates and photographs a nine millimeter casing on the floor, but he can't find any sign of the bullet.

Cheating Death
In autopsy, Dr. Robbins provides the answer to the puzzle of the missing bullet: it fragmented inside Janice's skull on impact. Suspicion falls heavier onto the husband, Willie Cutler, when they learn he recently lost his life savings in a gambling binge, visited a prostitute, and discovered his wife was having an affair.

EVIDENCE EVIDENCE EVIDE

PHONE KEYPAD
The phones in the Cutlers's home and Willie's office have blood on the 1 key, leading the CSIs to Sunstar Cabs, a company with the phone number 111-1111.

DESPERADO
Willie is found at his office surrounded by the dead bodies of his colleagues. Cutler claims that a shooter burst in and he played dead after being grazed by a bullet. CSI discovers Willie has a brother, Sammy, with a criminal record and who matches eyewitness descriptions from the crime scenes. When Dr. Robbins notices Willie faked his bullet wound, the guilt falls on Willie. Seeing no way out, Willie takes a hostage and holes up in a room at a casino. Unarmed, Brass goes in to negotiate with the killer.

Brother's Keeper

Willie insists that Sammy is responsible for the murders. Brass talks him into removing the gun from the hostage and aiming his sight at Brass instead. Brass bluffs, telling Willie that Sammy is downstairs and promises to get him on the phone. He appears to be making progress until Gil Grissom calls to inform him that Sammy Cutler has been dead for two months. At a stalemate, Brass calls out the safe word, "Jim," to alert the SWAT team. Willie shoots Brass twice. The SWAT team kills Willie, but Brass is gravely injured.

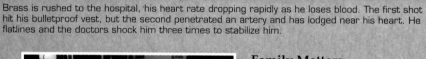

Brass is rushed to the hospital, his heart rate dropping rapidly as he loses blood. The first shot hit his bulletproof vest, but the second penetrated an artery and has lodged near his heart. He flatlines and the doctors shock him three times to stabilize him.

The surgeon tells Grissom, who holds the power of attorney for Brass, that the operation to remove the bullet could cause Brass to bleed to death. But without the surgery the bullet might migrate into his heart and kill him at any time. Grissom tells him to operate.

Family Matters

Grissom calls Brass's estranged daughter, Ellie, to tell her what's happened to her father. Ellie arrives at the hospital, her hostility palpable. She is convinced that everyone sees her as a worthless junkie, and raises eyebrows when she inquires about her father's pension.

A feeble Brass waves to the whole CSI team who has gathered outside the window of his hospital room

Close Call

Grissom shows Ellie the framed photo of her as a child that Brass keeps in his office. She retorts that it's easy for Brass to love the child she was and not the adult she has become. Nonetheless, she accompanies Grissom to the hospital and is visibly shaken when her father flatlines once again. Overcome with emotion, Ellie runs off before the doctors revive him. When Brass wakes up, he thanks Grissom for never giving up.

TIMELINE OF SEASONS

WHEN *CSI: CRIME SCENE INVESTIGATION* debuted on October 6, 2000, no one predicted how the show would change the landscape of television. Under the auspices of Jerry Bruckheimer, Carol Mendelsohn, Ann Donahue, and creator, Anthony E. Zuiker, *CSI* took viewers past the polite veneer of seemingly ordinary people's lives, past the glamour of Las Vegas, even past the thin layer of skin that covers a human body and into the dark underbelly of everyday life. Over six seasons, *CSI* has shown with an unflinching eye how investigators can tie a killer to a crime scene using a single hair or fiber and, in the process, draw millions of viewers each week to see how Grissom and his team use science to serve justice.

SEASON ONE

1.01 - PILOT

1.02 - COOL CHANGE

1.03 - CRATE 'N BURIAL

CSI recovers a woman, kidnapped and buried alive, but finds that she was a conspirator in the crime. Catherine and Warrick investigate a hit-and-run.

1.04 - PLEDGING MR. JOHNSON

When a woman's leg is found floating in a lake, her estranged husband and her lover are prime suspects. On campus, Nick and Sara examine the death of a fraternity pledge in a cruel "hazing" ritual.

1.05 - FRIENDS AND LOVERS

1.06 - WHO ARE YOU?

1.07 - BLOOD DROPS

1.08 - ANONYMOUS

1.9 - UNFRIENDLY SKIES

1.10 - SEX, LIES AND LARVAE

Entomology comes to the rescue when a battered woman shows up dead and her abusive husband looks to be guilty. The theft of a rare painting from a private collection uncovers a ring of art school counterfeiters.

1.11 - THE I-15 MURDERS

1.12 - FAHRENHEIT 932

1.13 - BOOM

1.14 - TO HALVE AND TO HOLD

1.15 - TABLE STAKES

1.16 - TOO TOUGH TO DIE

1.17 - FACE LIFT

1.19 - GENTLE, GENTLE

A small community is turned upside down when an infant is kidnapped. The whole CSI team work on the case. With no leads or apparant motives, suspicion turns towards the family after the baby turns up dead and evidence points too close to home.

1.21 - JUSTICE IS SERVED

1.23 - THE STRIP STRANGLER

A forensics savvy serial killer is terrorizing women in Las Vegas. The FBI takes charge of the investigation, and Grissom is removed from the case after accusing his superiors of placing politics before evidence. Sara offers to use herself as bait to catch the killer.

1.18 - $35K O.B.O.

1.20 - SOUNDS OF SILENCE

A deaf man is killed in what appears to be a hit-and-run. CSI feels the language barrier when trying to investigate the incident. Across town, a coffee shop massacre looks like a mob hit, but it may actually be an inside job.

1.22 - EVALUATION DAY

A case of a severed head found in the trunk of a car is, at first, thought to intersect with another case of a headless body found in the desert. Meanwhile, Warrick investigates the brutal killing of a young inmate at a local juvenile detention center.

SEASON TWO

2.01 - BURKED

2.02 - CHAOS THEORY

A freshman with plans to drop out of school suddenly drops out of sight. With several suspects, evidence reveals that a string of unrelated, accidental events caused her death.

2.03 - OVERLOAD

2.04 - BULLY FOR YOU

2.05 - SCUBA DOOBIE-DOO

Foul play collides with urban legend when a dead scuba diver is found up a tree. Across town, a bloody apartment isn't criminal, but leads CSI to a killer neighbor.

2.06 - ALTER BOYS

2.07 - CAGED

2.08 - SLAVES OF LAS VEGAS

2.09 - AND THEN THERE WERE NONE

2.10 - ELLIE

2.11 - ORGAN GRINDER

A real estate developer is found dead and redressed in a hotel elevator. Unfortunately, his widow has his organs harvested and his remains cremated before CSI can investigate.

2.12 - YOU'VE GOT MALE

2.13 - IDENTITY CRISIS

2.14 - THE FINGER

2.15 - BURDEN OF PROOF

2.16 - PRIMUM NON NOCERE

2.17 - FELONIOUS MONK

Four Buddhist monks are murdered, exposing motives of prejudice and greed in and outside the temple. Catherine uses new forensic techniques to solve a cold case in which her friend was murdered.

2.18 - CHASING THE BUS

2.19 - STALKER

2.20 - CATS IN THE CRADLE

2.21 - ANATOMY OF A LYE

2.22 - CROSS-JURISDICTIONS

2.23 - THE HUNGER ARTIST

SEASON THREE

3.01 - REVENGE IS BEST SERVED COLD

3.02 - THE ACCUSED IS ENTITLED

3.03 - LET THE SELLER BEWARE

3.04 - A LITTLE MURDER

Grissom suspects murder, rather than suicide, when a dwarf is found hanging during an International Organization of Little People convention. Meanwhile, Catherine is attacked by a perp while processing the scene of a robbery turned murder.

3.05 - ABRA CADAVER

3.06 - THE EXECUTION OF CATHERINE WILLOWS

3.07 - FIGHT NIGHT

3.08 - SNUFF

3.09 - BLOOD LUST

3.10 - HIGH AND LOW

3.11 - RECIPE FOR MURDER

3.12 - GOT MURDER?

The discovery of a human eye by a group of bird-watchers leads the CSI team down the trail to matricide in suburbia. In the morgue, Dr. Robbins and David Phillips are amazed to witness the shocking resurrection of the body of a poisoned car salesman.

3.13 - RANDOM ACTS OF VIOLENCE

3.14 - ONE HIT WONDER

3.15 - LADY HEATHER'S BOX

3.16 - LUCKY STRIKE

A peddler of "fool's gold" kills an irate customer and then manages to kill himself trying to cover his tracks. Elsewhere, the mother of a basketball player's child conspires in the kidnapping of one of the sports superstar's other children.

3.17- CRASH & BURN

3.18 - PRECIOUS METAL

3.19 - A NIGHT AT THE MOVIES

3.20 - LAST LAUGH

3.21 - FOREVER

3.22 - PLAY WITH FIRE

3.23 - INSIDE THE BOX

SEASON FOUR

4.01 - ASSUME NOTHING

4.02 - ALL FOR OUR COUNTRY

Two serial killers are killed by a vigilante court clerk before they can be brought to justice. A college student is found dead in his bathtub, having perished from a delayed head trauma.

4.03 - HOMEBODIES

4.04 - INVISIBLE EVIDENCE

4.05 - FEELING THE HEAT

A baby succumbs to extreme heat after being "accidentally" left in a car, a girl and her boating partner meet a watery grave, and a couch potato is electrocuted while trying to keep cool.

4.06 - FUR AND LOATHING

4.07 - JACKPOT

4.08 - AFTER THE SHOW

4.09 - GRISSOM VS. THE VOLCANO

4.10 - COMING OF RAGE

4.11 - ELEVEN ANGRY JURORS

4.12 - BUTTERFLIED

4.13 - SUCKERS

The theft of a counterfeit samurai sword unveils an elaborate insurance scam by a casino manager. Across town, a teenage girl is found exsanguinated in an abandoned house after a cultish vampire ritual.

4.14 - PAPER OR PLASTIC?

4.15 - EARLY ROLLOUT

4.16 - GETTING OFF

4.17 - XX

The body of a female inmate is discovered tied under a prison bus. The instigator was her jealous lover. Across town, a busted gambler stages his death so that his mentally challenged brother can collect his insurance.

4.18 - BAD TO THE BONE

4.19 - BAD WORDS

4.20 - DEAD RINGER

4.21 - TURN OF THE SCREWS

4.22 - NO MORE BETS

4.23 - BLOODLINES

SEASON FIVE

5.01 - VIVA LAS VEGAS

5.02 - DOWN THE DRAIN

5.03 - HARVEST

The staged murder of a teen girl leads CSI to a desperate family. A terminally ill brother euthanizes his sister who was born only to serve as his bone marrow donor.

5.04 - CROW'S FEET

5.05 - SWAP MEET

5.06 - WHAT'S EATING GILBERT GRISSOM?

5.07 - FORMALITIES

5.08 - CH-CH-CHANGES

CSI investigates the murder of a transgender woman who was threatening to expose the botched and butchered operations of a "surgeon" performing numerous illegal sex change procedures.

5.09 - MEA CULPA

5.10 - NO HUMANS INVOLVED

5.11 - WHO SHOT SHERLOCK?

5.12 - SNAKES

The decapitated head of an undercover journalist, writing a piece on Mexican music, is discovered in a newspaper dispenser. A wheelchair-bound senior citizen seeks revenge on a swindling telemarketer.

5.13 - NESTING DOLLS

5.14 - UNBEARABLE

Man and beast meet their end during a "canned hunt." Autopsy of the Kodiak bear reveals a missing gallbladder, implicating zoo workers for murder in order to sell organs on the black market.

5.15 - KING BABY

5.16 - BIG MIDDLE

5.17 - COMPULSION

5.18 - SPARK OF LIFE

5.19 - 4 X 4

5.20 - HOLLYWOOD BRASS

5.21 - COMMITTED

5.22 - WEEPING WILLOWS

5.23 - ICED

5.24 - GRAVE DANGER VOLS 1&2

SEASON SIX

6.01 - BODIES IN MOTION

The reunited CSI team piece together mysteries behind a trailer park explosion, a housewife-stripper found dead in a gutter, and how two decomposed bodies ended up in a car trunk.

6.02 - ROOM SERVICE

The pursuit of the American dream leaves a movie star and several immigrant laundry workers dead in this dark upstairs-downstairs look at the glitter and grime of Las Vegas.

6.03 - BITE ME

6.04 - SHOOTING STARS

6.05 - GUM DROPS

6.06 - SECRETS & FLIES

6.07 - A BULLET RUNS THROUGH IT, PART 1

6.08 - A BULLET RUNS THROUGH IT, PART 2

6.09 - DOG EAT DOG

An overweight man is found dead in a dumpster, taking CSI into the unappetizing side of competitive eating. Meanwhile, a couple involved in a bitter divorce are literally torn apart by man's best friend.

6.10 - STILL LIFE

6.11 - WEREWOLVES

6.12 - DADDY'S LITTLE GIRL

6.13 - KISS-KISS, BYE-BYE

A waiter is gunned down at a private party of an aging Sin City socialite. Motives abound until the hostess herself is found shot to death days later, turning the case in a completely different direction.

6.15 - PIRATES OF THE THIRD REICH

6.16 - UP IN SMOKE

6.14 - KILLER

The CSIs track down an ex-con when he tries to settle an old score, killing an innocent woman in the process and destroying the new life he had built.

6.17 - I LIKE TO WATCH

6.18 - THE UNUSUAL SUSPECT

6.20 - POPPIN' TAGS

When three teens are gunned down while posting bills to promote their favorite rapper, the CSI team is drawn into the violent drama of hip-hop street gangs.

6.22 - TIME OF YOUR DEATH

A movie producer's assistant is living the Vegas dream: winning big and getting the girl. When he is found dead, CSI discovers this "lucky streak" had unexpected origins.

6.19 - SPELLBOUND

In an occult shop, a psychic is murdered. All the material evidence suggests that her ability to see into the future of another's death could have been the cause of her own demise.

6.21 - RASHOMAMA

A high-profile attorney is murdered at her son's wedding. Despite differing interpretations of the blessed event, the team must piece together the case from memory after Nick's truck, containing the evidence, is stolen.

6.23 - BANG BANG

6.24 - WAY TO GO

GLOSSARY

A

Accelerant....a substance used to ignite and spread fire.

AFIS (Automated Fingerprint Identification System)....a computer database for fingerprint comparison.

Algor Mortis....the cooling down of a body after death.

ALS (alternate light source)....a high intensity (usually ultraviolet) illumination capable of detecting body fluids, fingerprints, and trace materials.

Asphyxia....lack of oxygen, a cause of death known commonly as suffocation.

B

Bindle....a sterile, folded paper or envelope used to transport evidence.

Biotoxin....a poisonous substance that comes from a living organism.

Blood Spatter....the dispersal pattern of blood resulting from a violent trauma.

Blower Brush....a dust applicator with a powder reservoir that charges a brush for applying fingerprint powder to large areas.

Buccal Swabs....DNA samples taken from the lining to the inner cheek.

Bunter Marks....etchings of a bullet's caliber and manufacturer on a casing.

C

Cadaver....a dead body.

Caliber....refers to the internal diameter of a gun barrel or of the bullet that fits a particular size gun.

Casing....the container in a round of ammunition, usually made of brass, steel, or plastic.

Casting....the preservation of an impression using plaster or another malleable substance to create a durable relief of physical evidence such as bite marks or tire treads.

Cast Off....blood spray emitted from the motion of a weapon.

COD....Cause of death.

CODIS (Combined DNA Index System)....an FBI database of DNA records from convicted offenders and crime scenes.

Core/Ambient Temperature....the temperature of a body in relationship to its environment; useful in determining time of death.

Cyanoacrylate fuming (glue fuming)....Fumes from heated glue are directed onto a surface using a fuming chamber and a small fan. Then fingerprint powder is applied to reveal prints.

D

DB....dead body.

Decomposition....the break down of tissues in a dead body influenced by bacteria, insects, and environmental conditions.

Denatured....changed the nature of.

DNA (deoxyribonucleic acid)....molecules found in every cell that are comprised of chromosomes; the typing of which is unique to every individual on earth.

Dual Comparison Microscope....allows simultaneous viewing of two separate objects juxtaposed in the same field for purposes of comparison.

E

Electronic Polymer Sensor Proboscis....a device that uses polymer plastics painted with conductive material to absorb and identify odors.

Electrostatic Dust Print Lifter....a device that deploys an electrostatic field to lift invisible dust prints from various surface types and enhance their visibility.

Epithelials....membranous tissue that covers most internal and external surfaces of the body and its organs.

ESDA (Electrostatic Detection Apparatus)....a device that utilizes powdered ink and a vacuum to reveal latent impressions on paper.

Exhumation....the digging up of a body after it has been buried.

Exsanguination....the draining of blood from a body.

F

Fluoroscope....a device that combines an X-ray machine and a fluorescent monitor to allow a view of the internal components in the body; utilized in searching for any foreign objects inside a corpse.

Follicular Tag....the bulb containing the pulp of a hair's root sheath cells, the presence of which can signify a struggle.

FTIR (Fourier Transform Infrared)....a form of spectroscopy that identifies organic and inorganic materials by measuring how the material absorbs various infrared light wavelengths.

Fuming....a method of raising latent prints from a surface by exposing it to the gas of acrylic resin; cyanoacrylate (super glue).

G

GC/MS (Gas Chromatograph/ Mass Spectrometer)....a device that separates a sample into individual components to analyze and identify molecular composition and chemical concentrations.

GSR....gunshot residue.

I

IBIS (Integrated Ballistics Imaging System)....a database that compares marking on a crime-scene bullet with bullets and weapons used in other crimes.

Instar....a stage in the life of an insect between two molts.

K

Kastle-Meyer Test....a rapid presumptive test, using the chemical compound phenolphthalein, to determine the presence of blood.

L

Latent Prints....a fingerprint that is not easily visible, and therefore requires processing, chemical or otherwise, to visualize the impression.

Lexis.com™....an online legal research database that includes federal and state codes, case summaries, and many other resources.

Ligature....a device used to bind or tie, commonly referred to as an instrument of strangulation.

Lividity....a discoloration of the skin caused by the gravitational settling of blood at time of death.

Locard's Theory....a principle that when two objects or people come into contact, there will be an exchange of material between them.

Luminol....a chemiluminescent compound that generates electromagnetic radiation (light) by the release of energy from a chemical reaction. Used to detect latent bloodstains by reacting with the hemoglobin in blood, causing the stain to glow.

M

Mikrosil™....a thick, silicone-based putty used for making molds.

MO (Modus Operandi)....meaning "method of operation," it refers to a criminal's characteristic pattern.

Muzzle Stamp....an abrasive impression inflicted on skin indicating a gun was held directly against the victim when fired.

N

Ninhydrin....a liquid or crystal substance that raises latent prints on paper and other porous surfaces by reacting with amino-acid residue in fingerprints.

O

OIS....officer-involved shooting.

P

Patent Print....visible prints found at a crime scene that can be lifted or photographed without additional processing.

PCR (Polymerase Chain Reaction)....a method for replicating smaller samples of DNA by mimicking cells to achieve a workable sample size.

Peri-mortem....around the time of, or during, death.

Petechial Hemorhaging.... also known as "Tardieu spots" freckle-like bruising caused by ruptured blood vessels that appear on the skin tissue, or in the eyes, of a victim of asphyxiation.

Phenolphthalein....a chemical reagent that, when mixed with hydrogen peroxide, detects the presence of blood indicated by a pink color change.

Polygraph....commonly known as a "lie-detector," this instrument measures changes in the human body to detect stress that may indicate a person is lying.

Precipitin Test....a "species of origin" test to determine whether or not a blood sample is human.

Projectile Trajectory Analysis....determining the path of an object though space using rods, strings, or lasers.

R

Reagent....any type of liquid or solid chemical used to produce a characteristic reaction during chemical analysis.

Ridge Details....the basic elements of a fingerprint (whorls, loops, and arches) which continue to form a unique pattern.

Rigor Mortis....the stiffening of a corpse, directionally from the head to the feet, starting at two to six hours after death.

Rubber Gelatin Lifters....an elastic sheet of rubber used to lift fingerprints, footprints, or shoe prints from smooth, hard surfaces.

S

SART (Sexual Assault Response Team)....typically nurses who collect a sexual assault evidence kit from a rape victim. The kit includes fluid samples, hair combings, fingernail scrapings, trace evidence, and photo documentation of wounds.

Scent Pad....used with police dogs, this is a sterile gauze filled with the scent of a person or object that is being searched for.

SEM (Scanning Electron Microscope)....this microscope can magnify very small details up to 500,000 times with high resolving power due to the use of electrons.

Sodium Rhodizonate....a chemical reagent that causes a color reaction used to identify the presence of GSR by detecting traces of lead.

SPR (Small Particle Reagent)....a chemical used to lift fingerprints that have been submerged in water.

Spectral Comparator....an instrument that uses different light wavelengths to identify properties of ink.

Spectrograph....a device used to measure and plot the wavelengths of light or sound.

STR (Short Tandem Repeat)....a method to obtain a DNA profile after replicating a small sample using PCR.

Striations.... microscopic scratches left by a tool on an item that it comes in contact with. A bullet is marked with striations as it passes through a gun's barrel.

Swab....sterile cotton fibers attached to the end of a wooden stick. An essential collection tool used to absorb trace fluid or dried stains for analysis.

T

Ten-Card....a paper and ink record of an individuals eight fingers and two thumbprints.

Tensometer....an instrument used by engineers to measure the tension, extension, and breaking point of a metal, rubber, or plastic sample.

Thermal Imaging Camera.... an infrared camera that senses the presence of heat, rather than light, to create a photographic image.

Thermocycler....alternates an increase and decrease in temperature to create a chain reaction that causes DNA to replicate.

Through-and-Through....a gunshot that passes though the dead body, creating both an entrance and exit wound.

TOD....time of death.

Trajectory....the course a projectile takes after being fired. Rods and lasers are used to recreate range and angle to determine the location of a shooter.

Tread Assistance™....a computer reference program that contains over 11,000 tire tread patterns.

V

VICAP (Violent Criminal Apprehension Program).... FBI database used to investigate cases of homicide and missing persons.

Vital Reaction....the swelling or red appearance in tissue which can be an indicator of trauma.

W

Walk-Through....the initial preliminary examination and evaluation of a crime scene.

Warrant....a court order empowering a law enforcement official to make an arrest, search, or seizure.

Y

Y Incision....the initiating cut in an autopsy that extends from both shoulders, meets in the sternum and continues downward over the abdomen to the pelvis.

INDEX

CSI: CRIME SCENE INVESTIGATION

Created by: Anthony E. Zuiker

Executive Producers: Jerry Bruckheimer, Carol Mendelsohn, Anthony E. Zuiker, Ann Donahue, Naren Shankar, Cynthia Chvatal, William Petersen, Jonathan Littman

EPISODE CREDITS

Page Numbers	Episode Name	#	Writer	Director
26–7	Jackpot	4.07	Naren Shankar & Carol Mendelsohn	Danny Cannon
32–3	Pilot	1.01	Anthony E. Zuiker	Danny Cannon
32–3	Anonymous	1.08	Eli Talbert & Anthony E. Zuiker	Danny Cannon
32–3	Identity Crisis	2.13	Anthony E. Zuiker & Ann Donahue	Kenneth Fink
36–7	Inside the Box	3.23	Carol Mendelsohn & Anthony E. Zuiker	Danny Cannon
42–3	The Execution of Catherine Willows	3.06	Carol Mendelsohn & Elizabeth Devine	Kenneth Fink
42–3	What's Eating Gilbert Grissom?	5.06	Sarah Goldfinger	Kenneth Fink
50–51	Random Acts of Violence	3.13	Danny Cannon & Naren Shankar	Danny Cannon
56–7	Gum Drops	6.05	Sarah Goldfinger	Richard J. Lewis
64–5	Butterflied	4.12	David Rambo	Richard J. Lewis
72–3	No Humans Involved	5.10	Judith McCreary	Rob Bailey
78–9	Crow's Feet	5.04	Josh Berman	Richard J. Lewis
88–9	Snuff	3.08	Ann Donahue & Bob Harris	Kenneth Fink
112–13	A Bullet Runs Through It, Part 1	6.07	Richard Catalani & Carol Mendelsohn	Danny Cannon
112–13	A Bullet Runs Through It, Part 2	6.08	Richard Catalani & Carol Mendelsohn	Kenneth Fink
116–17	Formalities	5.07	Dustin Lee Abraham & Naren Shankar	Bill Eagles
122–3	Slaves of Las Vegas	2.08	Jerry Stahl	Peter Markle
122–3	Lady Heather's Box	3.15	Teleplay by: Carol Mendelsohn & Andrew Lipsitz and Naren Shankar & Eli Talbert Story by: Anthony E. Zuiker & Ann Donahue and Josh Berman & Bob Harris	Richard J. Lewis
122–3	Pirates of the Third Reich	6.15	Jerry Stahl	Richard J. Lewis
124–5	Cross-Jurisdictions	2.22	Anthony E. Zuiker, Ann Donahue, Carol Mendelsohn	Danny Cannon
126–7	Grave Danger	5.24	Teleplay by: Anthony E. Zuiker Carol Mendelsohn Naren Shankar Story by: Quentin Tarantino	Quentin Tarantino
128–9	I Like To Watch	6.17	Henry Alonso Myers & Richard Catalani	Kenneth Fink
130–31	Bang Bang	6.23	Anthony E. Zuiker & Naren Shankar	Terrence O'Hara
130–31	Way To Go	6.24	Jerry Stahl	Kenneth Fink

ACKNOWLEDGMENTS

The publisher would like to thank the following for their kind permission to reproduce their illustrations:

Corbis: Al Francekevich 96-97; William Manning 20-21; Paul A. Souders 86-87; Getty Images: Digital Vision 60-61; MedioImages 46-47; Naoki Okamoto 60-61; Photodisc Green 38 39; Photolibrary: OSF 28-29; Science Photo Library: Kenneth Eward / Biografx 70-71; TEK IMAGE 74-75

The Publisher would also like to thank the following people:
Lynne Moulding for additional picture research
Razna Begum for additional permissions

Steve Parker would like to thank Caroline Pitt and Ben Horton

Photography:
Tony Esperaza
Bob Greene
Michael Kubeisy
Cliff Lipson
Paul Maples
Spike Nannarello
Robert Voets
Mark Wineman
Michael Yarish

Assistant in Writing and Research:
Kristine Huntley

VERY SPECIAL THANKS:

CBS Consumer Products
CSI Art Department
CSI Set Dressing Department
CSI Properties Department
Jerry Bruckheimer Television

Dominic Abeyeta
Dustin Abraham
Chris Barbour
Richard Berg
David Berman
Josh Berman
Paul Byers
Richard Catalani
Jenny Cheng
Mike Daley
Amy & Dean Davidson
Ann Donahue

Steven Felder
J.M. Finholt
Ken Fink
Carol Gable
Sarah Goldfinger
Andy Henry
Tom Hope
Jackie Hoyt
Matt Laudermilk
Jenn Levin
Richard Lewis
Fulvia Lindsay
Michael Lindsay
Racheal Luxenberg
Allen MacDonald
Missy McGuire
Ryan Mannix

Maryann Martin
Carol Mendelsohn
Louis Milito
Larry Mitchell
Daniel Novotny
Megan Pieper
David Rambo
Kristie Anne Reed
Que Reed
Mikelah Rose
Naren Shankar
Robyn Stewart
Kathleen Tanji
Sheila Thomas
Benjamin Tripp
Anthony E. Zuiker
Jon Wellner
and
Cast & Crew of CSI

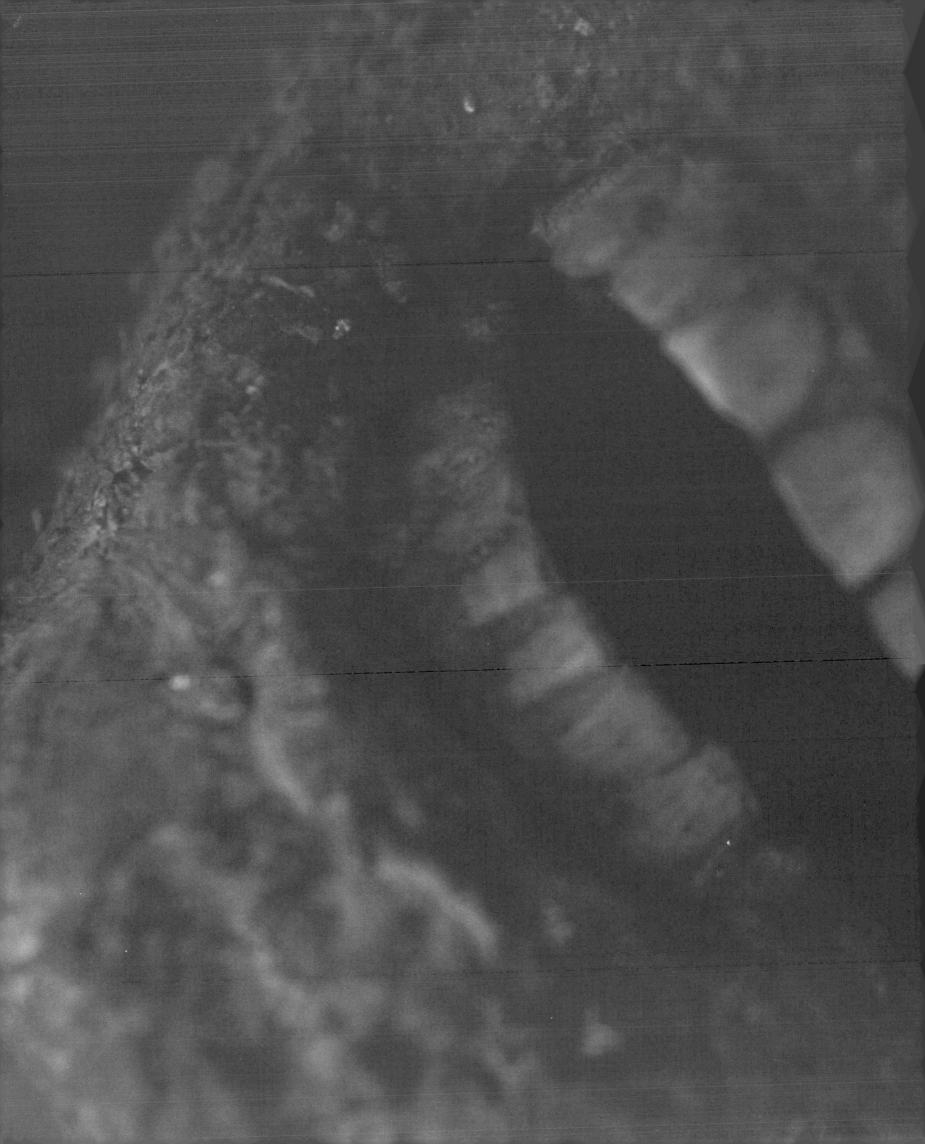